Table of Contents
Word Problems—Grade 2

FARM FUN

1. Farmer Jones collected 5 white eggs and 4 brown eggs from the chicken house. How many eggs did he collect in all?

2. The cows on the dairy farm gave enough milk every morning to fill 6 buckets. In the evening, they filled 4 buckets with milk. How many buckets of milk did they fill each day?

3. Lee picked 4 apples and Alex picked 3 apples. How many apples did they pick in all?

4. In the spring, 2 red colts and 2 spotted colts were born. How many colts were born in all?

5. The farmer tosses 3 bales of hay to his cows each morning and 3 more to them each afternoon. How many bales of hay do the cows eat each day?

6. The farmer's wife made 2 apple pies and one cherry pie for the fair. In all, how many pies did she make?

7. Mr. and Mrs. Finer bought 7 pounds of potatoes and 2 pounds of tomatoes at the farmer's roadside stand. How many pounds of vegetables did the Finers buy altogether?

8. Mother duck's 3 boy and 5 girl ducklings followed behind her in a line for their first swim in the pond. How many ducklings were there in all?

9. Nine crows sat on the farmer's fence, while one rested on the scarecrow in the garden. In all, how many crows were in the farmer's garden?

10. The farmer plowed 3 rows in which to plant corn and 2 rows in which to plant sunflowers. How many rows did the farmer plow?

HOW DO THEIR GARDENS GROW?

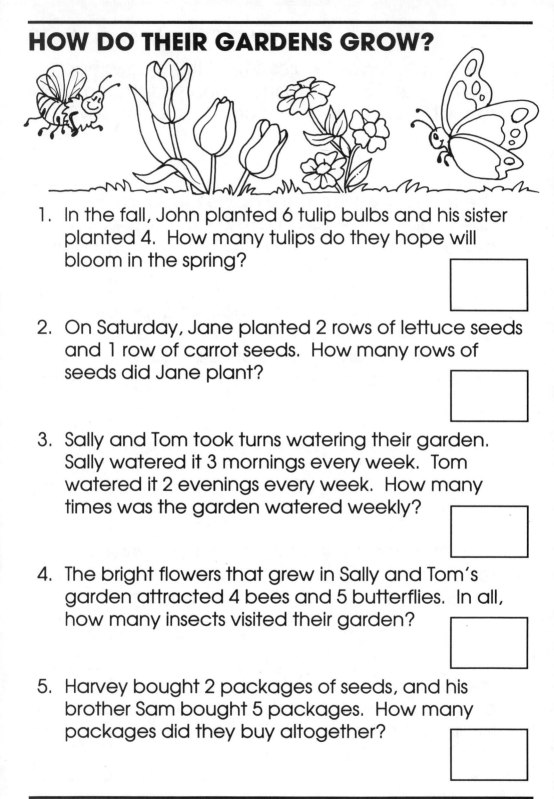

1. In the fall, John planted 6 tulip bulbs and his sister planted 4. How many tulips do they hope will bloom in the spring?

2. On Saturday, Jane planted 2 rows of lettuce seeds and 1 row of carrot seeds. How many rows of seeds did Jane plant?

3. Sally and Tom took turns watering their garden. Sally watered it 3 mornings every week. Tom watered it 2 evenings every week. How many times was the garden watered weekly?

4. The bright flowers that grew in Sally and Tom's garden attracted 4 bees and 5 butterflies. In all, how many insects visited their garden?

5. Harvey bought 2 packages of seeds, and his brother Sam bought 5 packages. How many packages did they buy altogether?

6. Martha and Joan picked flowers from their garden to give to Mother. Martha put 3 snapdragons in a vase. Joan added 6 daisies and put the vase on the table. How many flowers were in the vase?

7. The second-grade boys worked 5 hours preparing the students' garden plot. It took the girls 3 hours to plant the seeds and water them. How many hours were spent on the students' garden?

8. The students sold flowers for a penny apiece. Tony sold 4 zinnias and Peter sold 2 marigolds. How much money did Tony and Peter make?

9. Michael started his garden inside. When the weather was warm enough, he transplanted 5 tomato plants and 5 corn plants to a sunny spot in his yard. How many plants did Michael transplant?

10. Peggy saved her allowance all winter in order to buy rosebushes. In the spring, she bought 3 yellow rosebushes and 4 pink ones. How many rosebushes did Peggy buy?

COLLECTING IS FUN!

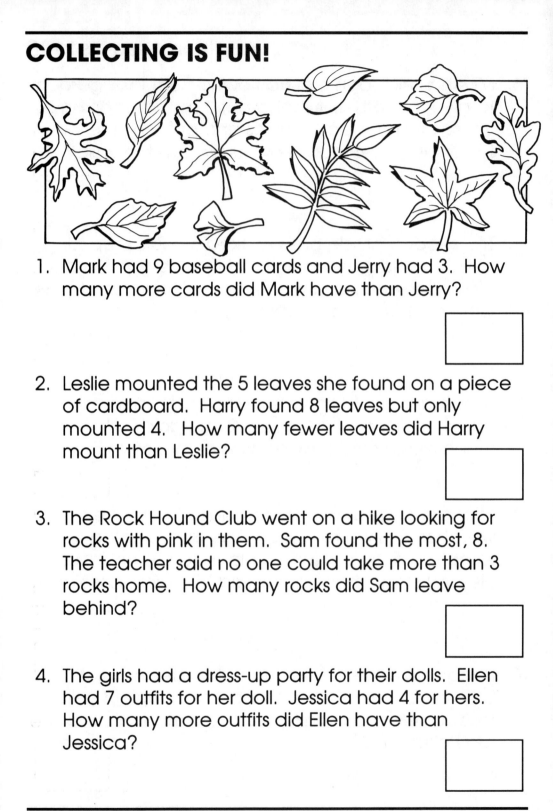

1. Mark had 9 baseball cards and Jerry had 3. How many more cards did Mark have than Jerry?

2. Leslie mounted the 5 leaves she found on a piece of cardboard. Harry found 8 leaves but only mounted 4. How many fewer leaves did Harry mount than Leslie?

3. The Rock Hound Club went on a hike looking for rocks with pink in them. Sam found the most, 8. The teacher said no one could take more than 3 rocks home. How many rocks did Sam leave behind?

4. The girls had a dress-up party for their dolls. Ellen had 7 outfits for her doll. Jessica had 4 for hers. How many more outfits did Ellen have than Jessica?

5. There were 10 fish in the aquarium. Four of them were angelfish. How many other fish were there?

6. Alex had 10 marbles. Alex gave Philip 3 marbles. How many marbles does Alex have now?

7. Anne and Barbara had a race at the beach to see who could find the most shells in 5 minutes. Anne found 5. Barbara found 8. How many fewer shells did Anne find than Barbara?

8. Sally collected 6 pine cones, and Marty found 8. How many more cones did Marty find than Sally?

9. Maggie collected a pencil from every place her family stopped on vacation. They stayed in 10 hotels. When she got home, she gave one to each of her 5 best friends. How many pencils did Maggie have left for herself?

10. Chris and Rick saved stamps. Chris had 7 stamps. Rick had 9. How many fewer stamps did Chris have than Rick?

HIGH FLIERS

1. Of the 7 kites in the air, 2 got tangled in trees. How many kites did not go into the trees?

2. The second-grade girls went to the park to fly 8 kites they had made. They were only able to get 5 of them in the air. How many kites were they unable to fly?

3. Mrs. Martin's class took 4 kites to the park, and Mr. Blackstone's class took 5. How many kites did the two classes take to the park altogether?

4. The second-grade boys flew paper gliders in the classroom. John's glider went the farthest. It landed 10 feet from its starting point. Pat's glider flew the shortest distance. It landed only 2 feet from its starting point. How many more feet did John's glider fly than Pat's?

5. Matt flew his remote-control model airplane around the park 4 times before it was forced to land. Tom flew his airplane around 6 times. How many times did their airplanes circle the park altogether?

6. Jane's dragon kite had 9 sections. Her brother's kite had 6. How many more sections did Jane's kite have than her brother's?

7. There were 3 blue kites and 7 red kites up in the sky. How many kites were up in the air altogether?

8. Dave's kite was one foot shorter than Rick's kite. Rick's kite was 5 feet long. How long was Dave's kite?

9. The girls counted 6 kites in the air. The boys counted 8. How many more kites did the boys count than the girls?

10. The class sent off 9 weather balloons. Each had a postcard attached asking each person who found a balloon to write on it where it was found and to mail it back. The class got 9 postcards back. How many balloons were never found?

HAPPY BIRTHDAY!

Miss Jolly's Students' Birthdays

Month	Students	Month	Students
January	🧍🧍🧍	July	🧍🧍
February	🧍	August	👧👧
March	🧍🧍👧	September	🧍🧍🧍👧
April	🧍👧👧👧	October	🧍🧍👧👧
May	🧍🧍👧	November	👧
June	🧍👧	December	

🧍 = one boy   👧 = one girl

1. How many students have birthdays in March and April?

2. How many boys have birthdays in September?

3. How many more students have birthdays in October than in February?

4. In which month do no students have a birthday?

5. Are there more boys or girls in Miss Jolly's class?

6. How many girls are in Miss Jolly's class?

7. How many students have birthdays during the summer (June, July, August)?

8. In which months do only boys have birthdays?

9. How many more girls have birthdays in April than girls have birthdays in June?

10. Which months have only 1 birthday?

THE PET SHOW

1. The student council sponsored a pet show. The council got several stores in town to donate 8 packages of dog food and 2 packages of cat food as prizes. How many packages of food were donated by the stores?

2. In preparing for the pet show, student council members read 7 books about running a pet show and 4 books about judging the pets. How many books did they read in all?

3. There were 3 golden retrievers and 8 Labrador retrievers shown in the hunting dog class. How many dogs were in this class?

4. In the classroom pet category, the students in first grade entered their aquarium containing 6 fish and their terrarium containing 5 chameleons. How many pets did the first-grade class enter in the show?

5. The pet owners in second grade won 9 blue ribbons and 3 red ribbons. How many ribbons did they win in all?

6. In the "Funniest Hat" contest, 5 dogs wore hats with flowers and 2 dogs wore hats with red, white and blue streamers. How many dogs were in the "Funniest Hat" contest?

7. In the "Good Manners" contest, the dogs had to sit and stand. Molly's dog, Rover, sat and stood the longest. Rover sat for 4 minutes and stood for 4 minutes. How many minutes did Rover sit and stand altogether?

8. There were 5 black cats and 5 spotted cats in the "Prettiest Cat" contest. How many cats were in this contest?

9. The fifth grade had the most cats entered in the show. Nine male cats and 3 female cats were entered from that grade. How many cats were entered from the fifth grade?

10. At the end, 4 cats and 8 dogs were judged for "Best Pet." How many pets were in the final event?

PARTY FUN

1. Kathy invited her entire class to her birthday party—
    9 boys and 8 girls including Kathy. How many
    children were at the party?

2. Kathy's cake had 7 pink candles and 2 blue
    candles on it. How many candles were on
    Kathy's cake?

3. There were 8 yellow balloons and 9 blue balloons
    taped to the center of the table. How many
    balloons were on the table?

4. Kathy counted out 8 orange jellybeans and 8
    yellow jellybeans for each guest's candy basket.
    How many pieces of candy did each guest get?

5. Danny got the most points in the beanbag toss game. He landed on the 9 square on his first throw and the 9 square on his second throw. How many points did Danny get altogether?

6. Tiffany found 5 squares and 9 triangles in the hidden shapes picture. How many shapes did she find altogether?

7. Kathy opened her presents. She got 13 books and 5 games. How many books and games did she get in all?

8. Kathy bought 6 red balls and 7 blue balls for the grab bag. How many balls were in the bag?

9. Wanda hopped 9 times on her right foot and 6 times on her left foot to win the hopping contest. How many times did she hop altogether?

10. Marty and Jason tied for first place in the "Penny Hunt." They each found 6 pennies. How many pennies did they find altogether?

BAKE SALE

1. Students signed up to make items for the bake sale. Haley said she would make 12 gingerbread cookies. Lori said she would make 8 butter cookies. How many more cookies did Haley make than Lori?

2. Erica made a cake for the bake sale. She cut it into 10 pieces. When the sale was over, 3 pieces remained. How many pieces of her cake were sold?

3. Bobby bought a cookie for 3 cents. He gave Ken a nickel. How many cents did Bobby get back?

4. Nancy bought a cupcake for 9 cents. She paid for it with a dime. How much money did she get back?

5. Carrie fell on her way to school and crushed 3 of the 6 loaves of banana bread she was taking to sell at the bake sale. How many of the loaves were still all right to sell?

6. The principal bought 10 cookies. He gave 6 of them to people in his office. How many cookies did he have left for himself?

7. Mary made a dozen (12) brownies. She kept 3 at home and took the rest to school for the bake sale. How many did she take to school?

8. There were 11 pies for sale. All but 2 sold. How many pies were sold?

9. Heather bought 7 cookies. She gave 4 of them away. How many were left?

10. Jeanne and Alexis bought a cake together. They cut it into 12 pieces. They saved 2 pieces for themselves. How many pieces did they give away?

SCHOOL SUPPLIES

1. The second grade began the year with 18 packages of drawing paper. At year's end, only 3 packages were left. How many packages of drawing paper had the students used during the year?

2. There were 16 students in the second grade and only 9 science books. How many students did not have a science book?

3. Jacob started the year with 12 new crayons. By winter break, he only had 7 of them left. How many crayons were no longer in Jacob's crayon box?

4. The teacher, Mrs. Gibbs, kept 10 pencils on her desk for students to use if they broke theirs during a test. After the spelling test, there were only 4 pencils left on her desk. How many pencils were used during the test?

5. Nine of the 17 desks in the room were old desks. How many desks were new?

6. The art teacher had 15 students at a time. She had 6 stencils for them to share. How many more students were there than stencils?

7. Each of the 18 classrooms had a wastebasket. At the end of the day, all but 3 were full. How many wastebaskets were full at the end of the day?

8. There were 14 computers in the back of the classroom. Six of them were in use. How many computers were not in use?

9. The school's lunchroom had 9 round tables and 4 square tables. How many more of the lunchroom tables were round than square?

10. Mr. Adams, the second-grade teacher, had 15 students in his homeroom. He offered to give each one a notebook, but only 8 of them took one. How many students did not take a notebook?

MOVING ALONG

1. Ted counted the cars on the freight train: 8 were tank cars; 18 were flat cars. How many more flat cars were there than tank cars?

2. Of the 19 bikes in the bicycle rack outside school, 4 of them were not locked. How many of them were locked?

3. Five fire engines and 2 ambulances sped to the scene of the accident. How many fewer ambulances went than fire engines?

4. Tony skated around the block 17 times while Jeff skated around it only 12 times. How many more times did Tony go around the block than Jeff?

5. Jenny jumped 12 times on a pogo stick before she fell off. Marianne was able to stay on for 15 jumps. How many less jumps did Jenny make?

6. Thirteen trucks at the terminal were loading fresh foods, and 8 trucks were loading paper supplies. How many less trucks were carrying paper items than fresh food?

7. There are times at Big City's airport when 15 airplanes take off in an hour, and only 3 trains leave its station during the same period. How many more airplanes take off in an hour than trains depart?

8. Eighteen cars began the race but only 14 of them finished. How many cars dropped out of the race?

9. The streets of the town seemed to shake when 14 members of the "Bumblebee Motorcycle Club" and 20 members of the "Spinning Tops Motorcycle Club" rode into town for a parade. How many more Spinning Tops were there than Bumblebees?

10. Tracy pushed her scooter down the street in 5 minutes. It took Susan 9 minutes to go the same distance. How much less time did Tracy go down the street than Susan?

COUNTING CARS

1. Jeff and Karen counted the number of vans they saw on the parking lot. Jeff counted 13. Karen counted 17. How many more vans did Karen see than Jeff?

2. There were 9 cars stopped at the light going west. There were 7 stopped at the light going east. How many cars were stopped at the light?

3. Mario loved sports cars. He saw 6 blue ones and 5 red ones drive down his street. How many sports cars did Mario see?

4. The car salesman had 4 cars and 9 vans to sell before the end of the month. How many more vans than cars did he have to sell?

5. Michelle saw 12 cars in front of school. Seven of them were decorated for the parade before the picnic. How many cars were not decorated?

6. The judges asked the 18 decorated cars to line up for judging. The judges gave ribbons to 9 of the cars. How many cars did not get a ribbon?

7. After the picnic, 7 cars were used to take food back to school, and 8 other cars took some students back to school. How many cars went back to school?

8. Two lines of cars were waiting to get into the park. There were 6 cars in one line and 8 in the other. How many cars were waiting to get into the park?

9. Sandy and Gina counted the number of cars that had out-of-state license plates. Gina saw 13. Sandy saw 8. How many more license plates did Gina see than Sandy?

10. Peggy went with her parents to look at new cars. They looked at 8 at The Car Stop and 4 at Adam's Auto Sales. How many more cars did they see at The Car Stop than at Adam's Auto Sales?

RIDE 'EM COWBOY!

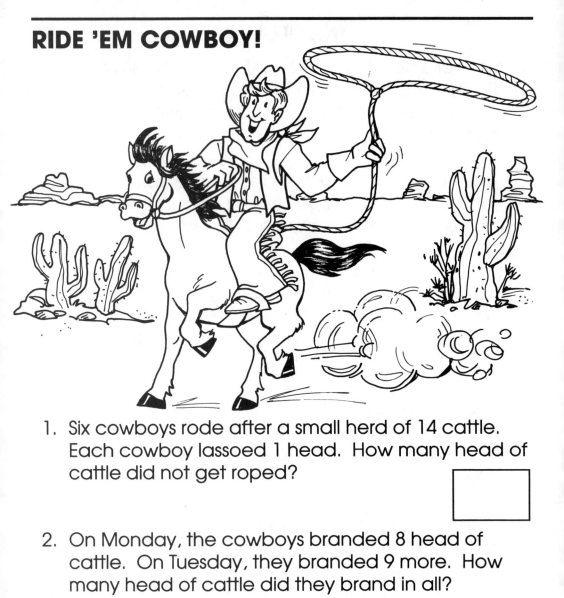

1. Six cowboys rode after a small herd of 14 cattle. Each cowboy lassoed 1 head. How many head of cattle did not get roped?

2. On Monday, the cowboys branded 8 head of cattle. On Tuesday, they branded 9 more. How many head of cattle did they brand in all?

3. The cowboys rounded up 20 horses for a trail ride. They put saddles on 12 of them. How many horses did not get saddled?

4. Of the 12 horses, 5 were spotted. How many horses did not have spots?

5. Three cowboys led 8 riders on the trail ride. How many people went on the trail ride altogether?

6. Of the 8 riders, only 2 had never been on a horse. How many riders had ridden a horse before the trail ride?

7. The riders saw 9 deer and 7 buffalo on the trail ride. How many deer and buffalo did they see altogether?

8. The cowboys packed a lunch for the group including 9 cans of soda and 9 cans of juice. How many cans of drink did they pack?

9. There were 6 cowboys from the area and 9 more that came from faraway ranches to be in the rodeo. How many cowboys were in the rodeo?

10. Only 2 cowboys out of 12 at the rodeo were able to ride the bucking bronco. How many cowboys were unable to ride it?

CLASS PROFILE

Hair Color	Boys							Girls						
Blonde														
Light Brown														
Dark Brown														
Red														
Black														
	1	2	3	4	5	6	7	1	2	3	4	5	6	7

1. How many boys have light brown hair?

2. How many more girls have dark brown hair than boys that have dark brown hair?

3. How many boys and girls have light brown hair?

4. How many students are in the class?

5. Are there more students in the class with light brown hair or dark brown hair?

6. How many boys have black hair?

7. How many more girls are in the class than boys?

8. How many boys and girls have blonde hair?

9. What color of hair does only 1 student have?

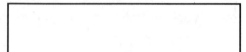

10. How many more boys have dark brown hair than blonde hair?

ANIMAL NOSE COUNT

Mrs. Harrow's second-grade class went on a field trip. They were told to count the number of animals they saw from the bus on the ride to the farm.

Animals We Saw

Name of Student	# of Pigs	# of Goats	# of Cows	# of Horses	# of Sheep
Sarah	2	1	6	2	2
David	6	1	5	4	4
Lisa	3	0	7	3	3
Josh	4	2	4	2	4
Madeline	3	1	9	3	2

1. How many fewer pigs did Madeline see than David?

2. Who saw the least number of pigs?

3. How many cows and horses did Josh see altogether?

4. How many fewer goats did Sarah see than cows?

5. How many cows did Lisa and Josh see together?

6. Who saw the most horses?

7. Who saw the same number of goats?

8. How many pigs and cows did Madeline see?

9. Who saw a total of 10 cows and horses?

10. How many horses did David and Lisa see together?

HERE COMES THE PARADE!

1. In this year's Tiny Town parade, there were 15 new floats plus 14 old ones that had already been in parades. How many floats were in this year's parade?

2. Eleven decorated bikes and 8 decorated wagons were entered in the children's section of the parade. How many bikes and wagons were there altogether?

3. Marching and dancing in front of Tiny Town's 81-piece band were its 16 cheerleaders and drum majorettes. How many members were there all together in the marching band?

4. There were 31 brass instruments and 24 woodwinds in the band. How many brass and woodwind instruments were there altogether?

5. There were 55 people on Main Street and 33 around the corner on Oak Street watching the parade. How many people were watching the parade in all?

6. The crowd cheered when 42 horses and their 42 riders trotted in step together in a straight line. How many horses and riders were there in the parade?

7. The pet section of the parade had 41 dogs and 37 cats in it. How many dogs and cats were in the parade?

8. A man selling balloons sold 26 red ones and 33 yellow ones. How many balloons did the man sell?

9. It took 60 people to make one of the floats. Thirty-two people rode on the float. How many people in all were responsible for making the float a success?

10. There were 55 flags and 13 banners in the parade. How many flags and banners were there in all?

SPORTING EVENTS

1. Two players on the Puffin basketball team were responsible for the team's win. One player scored 34 points, and the other scored 36. How many points did the players score altogether?

2. At halftime, the Puffins had 49 points. They scored 47 more in the second half. What was their final score?

3. The Hounds football team scored 28 points in the first half and 14 points in the second half. How many points did they score altogether in the game?

4. In the long jump, Jonathan Swift jumped 25 feet the first time and 28 feet the second time. How many feet did he jump altogether?

5. On 2 tries, Robert Strongarm threw the shot put 48 feet and 59 feet. How many feet did Robert throw the shot put altogether?

6. Steve Putter was the low scorer in the town's golf tournament. He turned in scores of 67 the first day and 69 on the second day. What was Steve's total score for the tournament?

7. The lady's winner in the golf tournament scored 74 the first day and 75 the second day. What was her total score in 2 days?

8. Two years in a row, Roger Puck was the leading scorer for the hockey team. He made 52 goals the first year and 49 the second year. What was the total number of goals Roger made in 2 years?

9. Jim and his brother went fishing in Alaska. Jim caught a 43-pound rainbow trout, and his brother caught one that weighed 38 pounds. How many pounds of trout did they catch altogether?

10. Hank Jones hit 44 home runs his first year of playing ball and 39 his second year. How many home runs did he hit in those 2 years?

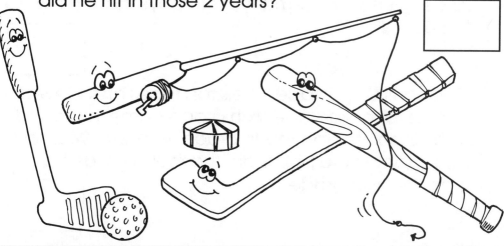

SCHOOL NUMBERS

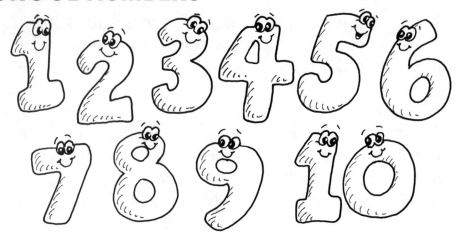

1. Of the 25 students in Mrs. Tiger's third-grade class, 22 of them were 8 years old. How many were not 8 years old?

2. Mrs. Rose's class had 24 students. Mr. Tool's class had 28. How many more students were in Mr. Tool's class than in Mrs. Rose's class?

3. There were 11 girls and 17 boys in the morning kindergarten. How many more boys than girls were there?

4. On Sports Day, grade levels ran races and played games for points. The sixth grade came in second with 72 points. The fourth grade won with 94 points. How many more points did the fourth grade have than the sixth grade?

Two-Digit Subtraction Without Borrowing

5. Eleven of the 51 first-graders were absent. How many first-graders were in school?

6. There were 62 sixth-graders and 69 fifth-graders. How many less students are in the sixth grade?

7. On Tuesday, 96 students brought their lunch and 53 bought their lunch. How many more students brought than bought their lunch?

8. At recess, the big playground had 55 students on it. The little playground had 35. How many fewer students were on the little playground?

9. The library had 35 new books. By the end of the day, all but 3 were checked out. How many books had been checked out?

10. There were 47 items in the lost and found. The principal hung them on a clothesline where students could see them. After school, 36 of the items were claimed. How many items remained in the lost and found?

DOWN BY THE WATER

1. During the winter, 25 geese made the lake their home. When spring came, 17 of them flew north. How many geese remained at the lake?

2. There were 83 lily pads in the pond and 46 of them had a flower. How many of the lily pads did not have a flower?

3. Bill was trying to step on each of the 36 stones in the water to cross over the stream. He stepped on 29 of them. How many stones did he miss?

4. Right now, 51 herons are in the marsh. At this time last year, there were only 12. How many more herons are in the marsh now?

5. Forty-seven alligators were in one area of the Everglades. Twenty-nine of them were asleep. How many alligators were awake?

6. One day, Philip counted 62 frogs in the pond. The next week, he counted 34. How many more frogs did Philip count the first time?

Tutor's Guide

This Tutor's Guide contains answer keys for Math Word Problems— Grade 2. Pull it out from the book to use as a guide.

FARM FUN

1. Farmer Jones collected 5 white eggs and 4 brown eggs from the chicken house. How many eggs did he collect in all? **9**

2. The cows on the dairy farm gave enough milk every morning to fill 6 buckets. In the evening, they filled 4 buckets with milk. How many buckets of milk did they fill each day? **10**

3. Lee picked 4 apples and Alex picked 3 apples. How many apples did they pick in all? **7**

4. In the spring, 2 red colts and 2 spotted colts were born. How many colts were born in all? **4**

Addition Answers to 10

5. The farmer tosses 3 bales of hay to his cows each morning and 3 more to them each afternoon. How many bales of hay do the cows eat each day? **6**

6. The farmer's wife made 2 apple pies and one cherry pie for the fair. In all, how many pies did she make? **3**

7. Mr. and Mrs. Finer bought 7 pounds of potatoes and 2 pounds of tomatoes at the farmer's roadside stand. How many pounds of vegetables did the Finers buy all together? **9**

8. Mother duck's 3 boy and 5 girl ducklings followed behind her in a line for their first swim in the pond. How many ducklings were there in all? **8**

9. Nine crows sat on the farmer's fence, while one rested on the scarecrow in the garden. In all, how many crows were in the farmer's garden? **10**

10. The farmer plowed 3 rows in which to plant corn and 2 rows in which to plant sunflowers. How many rows did the farmer plow? **5**

HOW DO THEIR GARDENS GROW?

1. In the fall, John planted 6 tulip bulbs and his sister planted 4. How many tulips do they hope will bloom in the spring? **10**

2. On Saturday, Jane planted 2 rows of lettuce seeds and one row of carrot seeds. How many rows of seeds did Jane plant? **3**

3. Sally and Tom took turns watering their garden. Sally watered it 3 mornings every week. Tom watered it 2 evenings every week. How many times was the garden watered weekly? **5**

4. The bright flowers that grew in Sally and Tom's garden attracted 4 bees and 5 butterflies. In all, how many insects visited their garden? **9**

5. Harvey bought 2 packages of seeds, and his brother Sam bought 5 packages. How many packs did they buy all together? **7**

Addition Answers to 10

6. Martha and Joan picked flowers from their garden to give to Mother. Martha put 3 snapdragons in a vase. Joan added 6 daisies and put the vase on the table. How many flowers were in the vase? **9**

7. The second-grade boys worked 5 hours preparing the students' garden plot. It took the girls 3 hours to plant the seeds and water them. How many hours were spent on the students' garden? **8**

8. The students sold flowers for a penny a piece. Tony sold 2 zinnias and Peter sold 2 marigolds. How much money did Tony and Peter make? **6¢**

9. Michael started his garden inside. When the weather was warm enough, he transplanted 5 tomato plants and 5 corn plants to a sunny spot in his yard. How many plants did Michael transplant? **10**

10. Peggy saved her allowance all winter in order to buy rose bushes. In the spring, she bought 3 yellow rose bushes and 4 pink ones. How many rose bushes did Peggy buy? **7**

COLLECTING IS FUN!

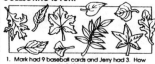

1. Mark had 9 baseball cards and Jerry had 3. How many more cards did Mark have than Jerry? **6**

2. Leslie mounted the 5 leaves she found on a piece of cardboard. Harry found 8 leaves but only mounted 4. How many fewer leaves did Harry mount than Leslie? **1**

3. The Rock Hound Club went on a hike looking for rocks with pink in them. Sam found the most, 8. The teacher said no one could take more than 3 rocks home. How many rocks did Sam leave behind? **5**

4. The girls had a dress-up party for their dolls. Ellen had 7 outfits for her doll. Jessica had 4 for hers. How many more outfits did Ellen have than Jessica? **3**

Subtraction 1-10

5. There were 10 fish in the aquarium. Four of them were angel fish. How many other fish were there? **6**

6. Alex had 10 marbles. Alex gave Philip 3 marbles. How many marbles does Alex have now? **7**

7. Anne and Barbara had a race at the beach to see who could find the most shells in five minutes. Anne found 5. Barbara found 8. How many fewer shells did Anne find than Barbara? **3**

8. Sally collected 6 pine cones, and Marty found 8. How many more cones did Marty find than Sally? **2**

9. Maggie collected a pencil from every place her family stopped on their vacation. They stayed in 10 hotels. When she got home, she gave one to each of her 5 best friends. How many pencils did Maggie have left for herself? **5**

10. Chris and Rick saved stamps. Chris had 7 stamps. Rick had 9. How many fewer stamps did Chris have than Rick? **2**

HIGH FLIERS

1. Of the 7 kites in the air, 2 got tangled in trees. How many kites did not go into the trees? **5**

2. The second grade went to the park to fly 8 kites they had made. They were only able to get 5 of them in the air. How many kites were they unable to fly? **3**

3. Mrs. Martin's class took 4 kites to the park, and Mr. Blackstone's class took 5. How many kites did the two classes take to the park all together? **9**

4. The second-grade boys flew paper gliders in the classroom. John's glider went the farthest. It landed 10 feet from its starting point. Pat's glider flew the shortest distance. It landed only 2 feet from its starting point. How many more feet did John's glider fly than Pat's? **8**

5. Matt flew his remote control model plane around the park 4 times before it was forced to land. Tom flew his around 6 times. How many times did their planes circle the park all together? **10**

6. Jane's dragon kite had 9 sections. Her brother's had 6. How many more sections did Jane's kite have than her brother's? **3**

7. There were 3 blue kites and 7 red kites up in the sky. How many kites were up in the air all together? **10**

8. Dave's kite was one foot shorter than Rick's. Rick's kite was 5 feet long. How long was Dave's kite? **4**

9. The girls counted 6 kites in the air. The boys counted 8. How many more kites did the boys count than the girls? **2**

10. The class sent off 9 weather balloons. Each had a postcard attached asking each person who found a balloon to write on it where it was found and to mail it back. The class got 9 postcards back. How many balloons were never found? **0**

Word Problems IF0181   9   ©Instructional Fair, Inc.

HAPPY BIRTHDAY!

Miss Jolly's Students' Birthdays

January	♂♂♂	July	♂♀
February	♂	August	♀♀
March	♂♂♀	September	♀♂♂♂
April	♂♂♀♂	October	♂♂♂♀
May	♂♂♀	November	♀
June	♂♀	December	

♂ = one boy   ♀ = one girl

1. How many students have birthdays in March and April? **7**

2. How many boys have birthdays in September? **3**

3. How many more students have birthdays in October than in February? **3**

4. In which month do no students have a birthday? **December**

Word Problems IF0181   10   ©Instructional Fair, Inc.

---

5. Are there more boys or girls in Miss Jolly's class? **boys**

6. How many girls are in Miss Jolly's class? **13**

7. How many students have birthdays during the summer (June, July, August)? **6**

8. In which months do only boys have birthdays? **Jan, Feb, & July**

9. How many more girls have birthdays in April than girls have birthdays in June? **2**

10. Which months have only one birthday? **February and November**

Word Problems IF0181   11   ©Instructional Fair, Inc.

THE PET SHOW

1. The student council sponsored a pet show. The council got several stores in town to donate 8 packages of dog food and 2 packages of cat food as prizes. How many packs of food were donated by the stores? **10**

2. In preparing for the pet show, student council members read 7 books about running a pet show and 4 books about judging the pets. How many books did they read in all? **11**

3. There were 3 golden retrievers and 8 Labrador retrievers shown in the hunting dog class. How many dogs were in this class? **11**

4. In the classroom pet category, the students in first grade entered their aquarium containing 6 fish and their terrarium containing 5 chameleons. How many pets did the first grade class enter in the show? **11**

Word Problems IF0181   12   ©Instructional Fair, Inc.

---

5. The pet owners in second grade won 9 blue ribbons and 3 red ribbons. How many ribbons did they win in all? **12**

6. In the "Funniest Hat" contest, 5 dogs wore hats with flowers and 2 dogs wore hats with red, white and blue streamers. How many dogs were in the "Funniest Hat" contest? **7**

7. In the "Good Manners" contest, the dogs had to sit and stand. Molly's dog, Rover, sat and stood the longest. Rover sat for 4 minutes and stood for 4 minutes. How many minutes did Rover sit and stand all together? **8**

8. There were 5 black cats and 5 spotted cats in the "Prettiest Cat" contest. How many cats were in this contest? **10**

9. The fifth grade had the most cats entered in the show. Nine male cats and 3 female cats were entered from that grade. How many cats were entered from the fifth grade? **12**

10. At the end, 4 cats and 8 dogs were judged for "Best Pet." How many pets were in the final event? **12**

Word Problems IF0181   13   ©Instructional Fair, Inc.

PARTY FUN

1. Kathy invited her entire class to her birthday party— 9 boys and 8 girls including Kathy. How many children were at the party? **17**

2. Kathy's cake had 7 pink candles and 2 blue candles on it. How many candles were on Kathy's cake? **9**

3. There were 8 yellow balloons and 9 blue balloons taped to the center of the table. How many balloons were on the table? **17**

4. Kathy counted out 8 orange jellybeans and 8 yellow jellybeans for each guest's candy basket. How many pieces of candy did each guest get? **16**

Word Problems IF0181   14   ©Instructional Fair, Inc.

---

5. Danny got the most points in the beanbag toss game. He landed on the 9 square on his first throw and the 9 square on his second throw. How many points did Danny get all together? **18**

6. Tiffany found 5 squares and 9 triangles in the hidden shapes picture. How many shapes did she find all together? **14**

7. Kathy opened her presents. She got 13 books and 5 games. How many books and games did she get in all? **18**

8. Kathy bought 6 red balls and 7 blue balls for the grab bag. How many balls were in the bag? **13**

9. Wanda hopped 9 times on her right foot and 6 times on her left foot in the hopping contest. How many times did she hop all together? **15**

10. Marty and Jason tied for first place in the "penny hunt." They each found 6 pennies. How many pennies did they find all together? **12**

Word Problems IF0181   15   ©Instructional Fair, Inc.

BAKE SALE

1. Students signed up to make items for the bake sale. Haley said she would make 12 gingerbread cookies. Lori said she would make 8 butter cookies. How many more cookies did Haley make than Lori? **4**

2. Erica made a cake for the bake sale. She cut it into 10 pieces. When the sale was over, 3 pieces remained. How many pieces of her cake were sold? **7**

3. Bobby bought a cookie for 3 cents. He gave Ken a nickel. How many cents did Bobby get back? **2¢**

4. Nancy bought a cupcake for 9 cents. She paid for it with a dime. How much money did she get back? **1¢**

Word Problems IF0181   16   ©Instructional Fair, Inc.

---

5. Carrie fell on her way to school and crushed 3 of the 6 loaves of banana bread she was taking to sell at the bake sale. How many of the loaves were still all right to sell? **3**

6. The principal bought 10 cookies. He gave 6 of them to people in his office. How many cookies did he have left for himself? **4**

7. Mary made a dozen (12) brownies. She kept 3 at home and took the rest to school for the bake sale. How many did she take to school? **9**

8. There were 11 pies for sale. All but 2 sold. How many pies were sold? **9**

9. Heather bought 7 cookies. She gave 4 of them away. How many were left? **3**

10. Jeanne and Alexis bought a cake together. They cut it into 12 pieces. They saved 2 pieces for themselves. How many pieces did they give away? **10**

Word Problems IF0181   17   ©Instructional Fair, Inc.

SCHOOL SUPPLIES

1. The second grade began the year with 18 packages of drawing paper. At year's end, only 3 packages were left. How many packages of drawing paper had the students used during the year? `15`

2. There were 16 students in the second grade and only 9 science books. How many students did not have a science book? `7`

3. Jacob started the year with 12 new crayons. By winter break, he only had 7 of them left. How many crayons were no longer in Jacob's crayon box? `5`

4. The teacher, Mrs. Gibbs, kept 10 pencils on her desk for students to use if they broke theirs during a test. After the spelling test, there were only 4 pencils left on her desk. How many were used during the test? `6`

Subtracting 1-18

5. Nine of the 17 desks in the room were old desks. How many were new? `8`

6. The art teacher had 15 students at a time. She had 6 stencils for them to share. How many more students were there than stencils? `9`

7. Each of the 18 classrooms had a wastebasket. At the end of the day, all but 3 were full. How many were full at the end of the day? `15`

8. There were 14 computers in the back of the classroom. Six of them were in use. How many were not in use? `8`

9. The school's lunchroom had 9 round tables and 4 square tables. How many more of the lunchroom tables were round than square? `5`

10. Mr. Adams, the second-grade teacher, had 15 students in his homeroom. He offered to give each one a notebook, but only 8 of them took one. How many did not take a notebook? `7`

MOVING ALONG

1. Ted counted the cars on the freight train: 8 were tank cars; 18 were flat cars. How many more flat cars were there than tank cars? `10`

2. Of the 19 bikes in the bicycle rack outside school, 4 of them were not locked. How many of them were locked? `15`

3. Five fire engines and 2 ambulances sped to the scene of the accident. How many fewer ambulances went than fire engines? `3`

4. Tony skated around the block 17 times while Jeff skated around it only 12 times. How many more times did Tony go around the block than Jeff? `5`

5. Jenny jumped 12 times on a pogo stick before she fell off. Marianne was able to stay on for 15 jumps. How many less jumps did Jenny make? `3`

6. Thirteen trucks at the terminal were loading fresh foods, and 8 trucks were loading paper supplies. How many less trucks were carrying paper items than fresh food? `5`

Subtraction 1-20

7. There are times at Big City's airport when 15 planes take off in an hour and only 3 trains leave its station during the same period. How many more planes take off in such an hour than trains depart? `12`

8. Eighteen cars began the race but only 14 of them finished. How many cars dropped out of the race? `4`

9. The streets of the town seemed to shake when 14 members of the "Bumblebee Motorcycle Club" and 20 members of the "Spinning Tops Motorcycle Club" rode into town for a parade. How many more Spinning Tops were there than Bumblebees? `6`

10. Tracy pushed her scooter down the street in 5 minutes. It took Susan 9 minutes to go the same distance. How much faster did Tracy go down the street than Susan? `4`

COUNTING CARS

1. Jeff and Karen counted the number of vans they saw on the parking lot. Jeff counted 13. Karen counted 17. How many more did Karen see than Jeff? `4`

2. There were 9 cars stopped at the light going west. There were 7 stopped at the light going east. How many cars were stopped at the light? `16`

3. Mario loved sports cars. He saw 6 blue ones and 5 red ones drive down his street. How many sports cars did Mario see? `11`

4. The car salesman had 4 cars and 9 vans to sell before the end of the month. How many more vans than cars did he have to sell? `5`

Addition and Subtraction 1-18

5. Michelle saw 12 cars in front of school. Seven of them were decorated for the parade before the picnic. How many were not decorated? `5`

6. The judges asked the 18 decorated cars to line up for judging. The judges gave ribbons to 9 of the cars. How many did not get a ribbon? `9`

7. After the picnic, 7 cars were used to take food back to school, and 8 other cars took some students back to school? `15`

8. Two lines of cars were waiting to get into the park. There were 6 cars in one line and 8 in the other. How many cars were waiting to get into the park? `14`

9. Sandy and Gina counted the number of cars that had out-of-state license plates. Gina saw 13. Sandy saw 8. How many more did Gina see than Sandy? `5`

10. Peggy went with her parents to look at new cars. They looked at 8 at The Car Stop and 4 at Adam's Auto Sales. How many more did they see at The Car Stop than at Adam's Auto Sales? `4`

RIDE 'EM COWBOY!

1. Six cowboys rode after a small herd of 14 cattle. Each cowboy lassoed one head. How many head of cattle did not get roped? `8`

2. On Monday, the cowboys branded 8 head of cattle. On Tuesday, they branded 9 more. How many head of cattle did they brand in all? `17`

3. The cowboys rounded up 20 horses for a trail ride. They put saddles on 12 of them. How many horses did not get saddled? `8`

Addition and Subtraction 1-20

4. Of the 12 horses, 5 were spotted. How many did not have spots? `7`

5. Three cowboys led 8 riders on the trail ride. How many people went on the trail ride all together? `11`

6. Of the 8 riders, only 2 had never been on a horse. How many had ridden a horse before? `6`

7. The riders saw 9 deer and 7 buffalo on the trail ride. How many deer and buffalo did they see all together? `16`

8. The cowboys packed a lunch for the group including 9 cans of soda and 9 cans of juice. How many cans of drink did they pack? `18`

9. There were 6 cowboys from the area and 9 more that came from faraway ranches in the rodeo. How many cowboys were in the rodeo? `15`

10. Only 2 cowboys out of 12 at the rodeo were able to ride the bucking bronco. How many cowboys were unable to ride it? `10`

CLASS PROFILE

HAIR COLOR	Boys	Girls
Blonde		
Light Brown		
Dark Brown		
Red		
Black		

1 2 3 4 5 6 7   1 2 3 4 5 6 7

1. How many boys have light brown hair? `7`

2. How many more girls have dark brown hair than boys have dark brown hair? `2`

3. How many boys and girls have light brown hair? `12`

4. How many students are in the class? `29`

5. Are there more students in the class with light brown hair or dark brown hair? `light brown hair`

6. How many boys have black hair? `0`

Tutor's Guide IF0181   C   ©Instructional Fair, Inc.

Reading a Bar Graph

7. How many more girls are in the class than boys?
1

8. How many boys and girls have blonde hair?
3

9. What color of hair does only one student have?
black

10. How many more boys have dark brown hair than blonde hair?
3

ANIMAL NOSE COUNT

Mrs. Harrow's second-grade class went on a field trip. They were told to count the number of animals they saw from the bus on the ride to the farm.

Animals We Saw

Name of Student	# of Pigs	# of Goats	# of Cows	# of Horses	# of Sheep
Sarah	2	1	6	2	2
David	6	1	5	4	4
Lisa	3	0	7	3	3
Josh	4	2	4	2	4
Madeline	3	1	9	3	2

1. How many fewer pigs did Madeline see than David?
3

2. Who saw the least number of pigs?
Sarah

Reading a Chart

3. How many cows and horses did Josh see all together?
6

4. How many fewer goats did Sarah see than cows?
5

5. How many cows did Lisa and Josh see together?
11

6. Who saw the most horses?
David

7. Who saw the same number of goats?
Sarah, David and Madeline

8. How many pigs and cows did Madeline see?
12

9. Who saw a total of 10 cows and horses?
Lisa

10. How many horses did David and Lisa see together?
7

HERE COMES THE PARADE!

1. In this year's Tiny Town parade, there were 15 new floats plus 14 old ones that had been in parades before. How many floats were in this year's parade?
29

2. Eleven decorated bikes and 8 decorated wagons were entered in the children's section of the parade. How many bikes and wagons were there all together?
19

3. Marching and dancing in front of Tiny Town's 81-piece band were its 16 cheerleaders and drum majorettes. How many members were there all together in the marching band?
97

4. There were 31 brass instruments in the band and 24 woodwinds. How many brass and woodwind instruments were there all together?
55

Two-Digit Addition Without Carrying

5. There were 55 people on Main Street and 33 around the corner on Oak Street watching the parade. How many people were watching the parade in all?
88

6. The crowd cheered when 42 horses and their 42 riders trotted in step together in a straight line. How many horses and riders were there in the parade?
84

7. The pet section of the parade had 41 dogs and 37 cats in it. How many dogs and cats were in the parade?
78

8. A man selling balloons sold 26 red ones and 33 yellow ones. How many balloons did the man sell?
59

9. It took 60 people to make one of the floats. Thirty-two people rode on the float. How many people in all were responsible for making the float a success?
92

10. There were 55 flags and 13 banners in the parade. How many flags and banners were there in all?
68

SPORTING EVENTS

1. Two players on the Puffin's basketball team were responsible for the team's win. One scored 34 points, and the other scored 36. How many points did the two players score?
70

2. At halftime, the Puffins had 49 points. They scored 47 more in the second half. What was their final score?
96

3. The Hounds football team scored 28 points in the first half and 14 points in the second half. How many points did they score all together in the game?
42

4. In the long jump, Jonathan Swift jumped 25 feet the first time and 28 feet the second time. How many feet did he jump all together?
53

5. On two tries, Robert Strongarm threw the shot put 48 feet and 59 feet. How many feet did Robert throw the shot put all together?
107

6. Steve Putter was the low scorer in the town's golf tournament. He turned in scores of 67 the first day and 69 on the second day. What was Steve's total score for the two days?
136

Two-Digit Addition With Carrying

7. The lady's winner in the golf tournament scored 74 the first day and 75 the second day. What was her total score in two days?
149

8. Two years in a row, Roger Puck was the leading scorer for the hockey team. He made 52 goals the first year and 49 the second year. What was the total number of goals Roger made in two years?
101

9. Jim and his brother went fishing in Alaska. Jim caught a 43 pound rainbow trout, and his brother caught one that weighed 38 pounds. How many pounds of trout did they catch all together?
81

10. Hank Jones hit 44 home runs his first year of playing ball and 39 his second year. How many home runs did he hit in those two years?
83

SCHOOL NUMBERS

1. Of the 25 students in Mrs. Tiger's third-grade class, 22 of them were eight years old. How many were not eight years old?
3

2. Mrs. Rose's class had 24 students. Mr. Tool's class had 28. How many more students were in Mr. Tool's class than in Mrs. Rose's class?
4

3. There were 11 girls and 17 boys in the morning kindergarten. How many more boys than girls were there?
6

4. On Sports Day, grade levels ran races and played games for points. The sixth grade came in second with 72 points. The fourth grade won with 94 points. How many more points did the fourth grade have than the sixth grade?
22

Two-Digit Subtraction Without Borrowing

5. Eleven of the 51 first graders were absent. How many first-graders were in school?
40

6. There were 62 sixth-graders and 69 fifth-graders. How many less students are in the sixth grade?
7

7. On Tuesday, 96 students brought their lunch and 53 bought their lunch. How many more students brought than bought their lunch?
43

8. At recess, the big playground had 55 students on it. The little playground had 35. How many fewer students were on the little playground?
20

9. The library had 35 new books. By the end of the day, all but 3 were checked out. How many had been checked out?
32

10. There were 47 items in the lost and found. The principal hung them on a clothesline where students could see them. After school, 36 of the items were claimed. How many items remained in the lost and found?
11

DOWN BY THE WATER

1. During the winter, 25 geese made the lake their home. When spring came, 17 of them flew north. How many geese remained at the lake? **8**

2. There were 83 lily pads in the pond and 46 of them had a flower. How many of the lily pads did not have a flower? **37**

3. Bill was trying to step on each of the 36 stones in the water to cross over the stream. He stepped on 29 of them. How many stones did he miss? **7**

4. Right now, 51 herons are in the marsh. At this time last year, there were only 12. How many more herons are in the marsh now? **39**

5. Forty-seven alligators were in one area of the Everglades. Twenty-nine of them were asleep. How many were awake? **18**

6. One day, Philip counted 62 frogs in the pond. The next week, he counted 34. How many more frogs did Philip count the first time? **28**

Word Problems #0181   36   ©Instructional Fair, Inc.

Two-Digit Subtraction With Borrowing

7. Of the 94 cottonwood and willow trees that lined the banks of the stream, 45 of them were cottonwoods. How many were willow trees? **49**

8. The fisherman was out in his boat all day. He had 42 "bites," but he caught only 5 fish. How many of his "bites" got away or weren't fish? **37**

9. Nathan had 33 fish in his aquarium. He especially liked the 14 fish with bright colors. How many fish did he have that were not brightly colored? **19**

10. Seventy-four seagulls sat on the pier that stretched out into the lake. When a large school of fish swam past, 59 seagulls flew after them. How many seagulls remained on their perches on the pier? **15**

Word Problems #0181   37   ©Instructional Fair, Inc.

CARNIVAL FUN

1. There were 23 shows and 15 games at the carnival. How many activities were at the carnival? **38**

2. Benjamin tried to win a basketball by getting at least 70 points throwing 2 beanbags. He got 25 points with the first bag he threw and 37 with the second. How many points did Benjamin get? **62**

3. Gordie worked at the snow cone booth. He served 54 grape snow cones and 31 lemon snow cones. How many more grape snow cones did he serve? **23**

4. There were 14 elephants and 23 monkeys in the animal show. How many animals were in the show? **37**

5. Peter started out with 25 tickets. Within the first hour, he had used 17 of them. How many tickets did he have left? **8**

6. The merry-go-round could hold 56 people. There were 44 on it. How many more people could get on the merry-go-round? **12**

Word Problems #0181   38   ©Instructional Fair, Inc.

Two-Digit Addition and Subtraction

7. Two small cars drove into the tent. Sixteen clowns got out of one car; 22 got out of the other car. How many clowns got out of the two cars? **38**

8. Jamie took a guess at how many candles were in the jar. He guessed 57. There were 76. By how many did Jamie miss the correct number? **19**

9. There were 37 white mice and 12 black mice in the mouse show. How many mice were in the mouse show? **49**

10. Taylor played the dart game. He started with 99 points. The object of the game was to get down to zero. He threw three darts for a total of 67 points. How many more points did he need to get to zero? **32**

Word Problems #0181   39   ©Instructional Fair, Inc.

ECOLOGY COUNT

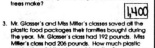

1. John and Mike collected used newspapers in their neighborhood for the scout paper drive. John brought in 253 pounds of paper, and Mike brought in 144 pounds. How many pounds of paper did they collect all together? **397**

2. Trees are used to make paper. One tree could make 700 paper grocery bags. What could two trees make? **1,400**

3. Mr. Glasser's and Miss Miller's classes saved all the plastic food packages their families bought during the year. Mr. Glasser's class had 192 pounds. Miss Miller's class had 206 pounds. How much plastic packaging did they have all together? **398**

4. While riding in the car, Murray counted 256 pieces of trash along the roadside the first day of his vacation. His brother counted 223 pieces the second day. How many pieces of trash did they count all together? **479**

Word Problems #0181   40   ©Instructional Fair, Inc.

Three-Digit Addition Without Carrying

5. The sixth grade separated the plastic and glass bottles and jars they collected. The sixth-graders counted 121 glass containers and 352 plastic ones. How many bottles and jars did they collect? **473**

6. Katie and her family used 175 feet of paper towels one week. The next week, they tried to use less. They only used 122 feet. How many feet of paper towels did they use both weeks? **297**

7. Martin and Harris saved all the junk mail delivered to their homes in a month. Martin got 216 pieces of junk mail. Harris got 310. How many pieces of junk mail did they receive all together? **526**

8. Teri counted the number of times her refrigerator door was opened every day. At the end of the month, it had been opened 506 times. Loni did the same at her house and found hers was opened 483 times. How many times did their refrigerator doors open all together? **989**

9. By letting the water run when she washed the dishes, Mother wasted at least 210 gallons of water in a week. How many gallons of water did she waste in two weeks? **420**

Word Problems #0181   41   ©Instructional Fair, Inc.

WEIGH IN

1. The total weight of the boys in the class was 952 pounds. The total weight of the girls was 770. What was the total weight of the class? **1,722**

2. Mrs. Joseph, the principal, weighed 137 pounds. Her secretary weighed 115. What did they weigh together? **252**

3. The school nurse made a chart with the total weight of each grade level. The first grade weighed 968 pounds, and the kindergarten weighed 857 pounds. How much did the two grade levels weigh together? **1,825**

4. Mrs. Leap's room collected 206 pounds of newspaper, and Mrs. Bound's room collected 329 pounds. How many pounds of paper did the two rooms collect all together? **535**

Word Problems #0181   42   ©Instructional Fair, Inc.

Three-Digit Addition With Carrying

5. The boxers weighed in before their match. One weighed 404 pounds. The other weighed 397 pounds. How much did they weigh together? **801**

6. The mother elephant had two babies. One weighed 105 pounds. The other weighed 109 pounds. How much did they weigh all together? **214**

7. The mother bear weighed 927 pounds. Her cub weighed 143 pounds. How much did they weigh all together? **1,070**

8. The zoo used 550 pounds of hay just for the elephants in a day. How much did they use in 2 days? **1,100**

9. The pet store sold 156 pounds of dog food in the morning and 191 pounds in the afternoon. How much dog food did the store sell all day? **347**

10. The pet store had 109 pounds of dog food left. The store ordered 959 pounds more. How much would it then have all together? **1,068**

Word Problems #0181   43   ©Instructional Fair, Inc.

CROWD CONTROL

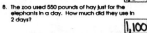

1. The movie theater held only 785 people. There were 995 people wanting to see the movie. How many people did the theater have to turn away? **210**

2. The pet store had 566 mice. There were only enough cages for 450. How many mice did the store have to give away? **116**

3. The dog and cat shelter had 678 animals. The shelter really could hold only 425 at a time. How many dogs and cats did they need to quickly find homes for? **253**

4. In the low part of the forest, 825 trees were crowded together so that none of them were growing very well. The forest service moved 304 of the trees to other parts of the forest. How many trees remained in the low part? **521**

Word Problems #0181   44   ©Instructional Fair, Inc.

Tutor's Guide IF0181   E   ©Instructional Fair, Inc.

Three-Digit Subtraction Without Borrowing

5. After the football game, 473 excited fans ran onto the field. The ushers had to remove 162 of them who were tearing down the goal posts. How many fans got to remain on the field?

    `311`

6. Trucks came to the feed lot to pick up some of the 975 cattle waiting to be shipped to market. The trucks were able to take all but 152 of the cattle. How many cattle went on the trucks?

    `823`

7. The store counted 879 shirts when it took inventory. The store decided to put 354 of them on sale. How many shirts did not go on sale?

    `525`

8. One day, the library checked out 315 books and checked in 568 returns. How many more books were returned than checked out?

    `253`

9. The museum guards let in only 125 people of the 686 waiting in line to see the exhibit. How many people were still in line?

    `561`

10. There were 156 new cars available and 266 buyers. How many buyers had to wait for the next shipment of cars?

    `110`

Word Problems #0181   45   ©Instructional Fair, Inc.

MAXIMUM AND MINIMUM

1. The sign on the bridge read, "No more than 150 people may stand on this bridge at one time." There were 203 people on it. How many people had to get off the bridge?

    `53`

2. When James hit the muscle machine with a sledge hammer, the bell went off because he got the most points possible—990. Harvey got only 399 points. How many more points did James get than Harvey?

    `591`

3. The highest building in downtown Higginsville had 810 steps from the ground floor to the fortieth floor on top. The shortest building had only 125 steps. How many more steps did the tallest building have than the shortest?

    `685`

4. Toby read the most pages, 946, during free reading time. Stan read the least, 209. How many more pages did Toby read than Stan?

    `737`

5. While practicing for the race, Jack kept a record of how long it took him to run 26 miles. His best time was 390 minutes. His worst time was 425 minutes. What is the difference between his best and worst times?

    `35`

Word Problems #0181   46   ©Instructional Fair, Inc.

Three-Digit Subtraction With Borrowing

6. The highest hill in the park is 352' high. The smallest hill is 196' high. What is the difference in height between the two hills?

    `156`

7. The students at Central School were saving energy. They had a contest to see who walked the most miles. Greg won. He walked 437 miles. Louis walked the least. He walked 59 miles. What was the difference between the boys' miles?

    `378`

8. Theo raised the most money, $8.27, for the class present to the school. Penny raised the least, $1.59. What was the difference between the amounts?

    `$6.68`

9. The grade level with the most students was sixth grade. It had 305 students. The grade level with the least number of students was second grade. It had 269. What was the difference between the number of students in the two grades?

    `36`

10. The largest factory in town had 685 people working in it. The smallest factory had 96. What is the difference in the number of people employed in the largest and smallest factories?

    `589`

Word Problems #0181   47   ©Instructional Fair, Inc.

OVER THE RIVER AND THROUGH THE WOODS

OCEAN 356 miles

1. On the first day of the Diamond's vacation to the ocean, they drove 427 miles. On the second day, they drove 356 miles. How far was the ocean from their home?

    `783`

2. The furniture left the factory on a freight train. It traveled 605 miles before it was put on a truck. The truck drove 419 miles to the store. How far did the furniture travel until it reached its destination?

    `1,024`

3. Tim's grandparents lived 756 miles from him. If they drove 314 miles the first day of their trip, how far would they have to drive the second day to reach Tim's house?

    `442`

4. The Murrays and Sheelines were friends, but they lived far apart. They decided to meet in a city almost halfway between them. The Murrays drove 389 miles, and the Sheelines drove 398 miles. How many miles apart did they live?

    `787`

Word Problems #0181   48   ©Instructional Fair, Inc.

Three-Digit Addition and Subtraction

5. The train had to travel 890 miles. It had gone 512 miles. How much farther did it have to go?

    `378`

6. The Bakers had 692 miles to travel. They stopped for lunch after going 293 miles. How many miles did they have to go after lunch?

    `399`

7. Mrs. Saff drove 129 miles, and her husband drove 205 miles. How far did they drive all together?

    `334`

8. The airplane was scheduled to land once before it reached its destination of Chicago which was 545 miles away. It landed in St. Louis after flying 255 miles. How many more miles did the plane have to travel before it arrived in Chicago?

    `290`

9. The three-day cruise was 744 miles. The ship's last stop was 578 miles from its final port. How many miles did the ship have left to travel?

    `166`

10. Lenny drove back and forth to work five days a week for a total of 192 miles. His boss drove a total of 180 miles a week. How many miles did they drive all together?

    `372`

Word Problems #0181   49   ©Instructional Fair, Inc.

BIG, BIGGER, BIGGEST

1. Shawna is 47" tall. Her little sister is 32" tall. How much taller is Shawna than her little sister?

    `15"`

2. Max's sofa is 6'4" long and his chair is 3'3" wide. If he puts them side by side along a wall, how many feet and inches will they be together?

    `9'7"`

3. The rug in the playroom needs to be replaced. Two of its sides are 72" each, and the other two sides are 100" each. What is the perimeter of the rug?

    `344"`

4. Julie, Geri and Betsy walked in the walkathon to raise money for a new library. Julie walked 11 miles, Geri walked 15, and Betsy walked 9. How many miles did they walk all together?

    `35`

Word Problems #0181   50   ©Instructional Fair, Inc.

Addition and Subtraction Using Measures

5. Andy weighed 45 pounds last year and was 3'5" tall. When he was measured this year, he weighed 59 pounds and was 3'10" tall. How many pounds did he gain and how many inches did he grow in one year?

    `14 lbs, 5"`

6. Aaron weighed more than anyone else in the class. He weighed 87 pounds. Sue weighed the least. She weighed 46 pounds. What was the difference in their weights?

    `41 lbs`

7. If today were the sixth of October, how many days would it be until the eighteenth?

    `12`

8. The first of April is on a Sunday. What will the date of the next Sunday be?

    `8`

9. In the morning, the temperature was 32 degrees. In the afternoon, it rose to 60 degrees. How many degrees warmer was it in the afternoon?

    `28°`

10. There are 2 cups in a pint. There are 2 pints in a quart. How many cups are in a quart?

    `4`

Word Problems #0181   51   ©Instructional Fair, Inc.

SPRING CONCERT

1. There were 6 violins, 4 cellos and 2 bass instruments in the string section of the orchestra. How many string instruments were in the orchestra?

    `12`

2. There were 2 tubas, 4 trombones and 4 trumpets in the brass section. How many instruments were in the brass section?

    `10`

3. The woodwind section had 6 clarinet players, 3 oboe players and 5 bassoon players. How many players were in the woodwind section?

    `14`

4. The percussion section was the smallest section but perhaps the loudest. It had 1 piano, 2 drums and one tambourine. How many instruments were in the percussion section of the orchestra?

    `4`

Word Problems #0181   52   ©Instructional Fair, Inc.

Three Single-Digit Addends

5. The singers in the first row held 7 tulips, 5 daisies and 8 roses. How many flowers were held by the singers in the first row?

    `20`

6. The girls wore light-colored dresses. Eight wore pink, 9 wore yellow and 9 wore light blue. How many girls wore light-colored dresses?

    `26`

7. The program listed 3 dances, 8 songs and 7 musical pieces to be performed. How many items were listed on the program?

    `18`

8. The first dance took 3 minutes, the second took 5 minutes, and the last dance took 3 minutes. How many minutes long were the dances?

    `11`

9. There were refreshments after the concert. Carrie had 3 cookies, her brother had 3, and her mom had 2. How many cookies did Carrie and her family eat?

    `8`

10. The boys in the chorus had 9 glasses of grape juice, 9 glasses of lemonade and 9 glasses of punch. How many drinks did the boys have in all?

    `27`

Word Problems #0181   53   ©Instructional Fair, Inc.

Tutor's Guide IF0181   F   ©Instructional Fair, Inc.

COUNTING ON VACATION

1. The Cutlers traveled by car to visit Grandma. Mother packed 12 pairs of jeans, 24 T-shirts and 10 sweaters for the family. How many things did she pack?

46

2. Lawrence Cutler amused himself on the trip by counting out-of-state license plates. He saw 11 from New Mexico, 12 from Colorado and 10 from Arizona. How many license plates did Lawrence count?

33

3. Nan Cutler counted the number of farm animals she saw. She counted 35 cows, 12 horses and 15 pigs. How many farm animals did she count?

62

4. In the first hour, the Cutlers traveled 45 miles. In the second hour, they traveled 52 miles. In the third hour, they traveled 16 miles. How many miles did they travel during the first three hours of the trip?

113

Three Two-Digit Addends

5. The Cutlers filled the car with 18 gallons of gas before they left home. They filled it again with 15 gallons and again with 17 gallons. How many gallons did they fill the car with all together on the trip?

50

6. Lawrence swam laps in his grandmother's pool. One day, he swam 16 laps. The next day, he swam 21 laps, and the last day, he swam 33 laps. How many laps did Lawrence swim in all?

70

7. Nan helped Grandma bake cookies. They made 46 sugar cookies, 36 chocolate cookies and 25 butter cookies. How many cookies did they make?

107

8. Every day, the Cutlers had quiet time. They watched TV for 60 minutes. They read for 25 minutes, and they played a game for 45 minutes. How many minutes of their day was spent doing something quiet?

130

9. The Cutler family took a short side trip. They drove 41 miles to the ocean. Then they drove along the coast for 14 miles. The trip back to Grandma's house was 48 miles. How many miles in all was their side trip?

103

COUNTING MONEY

1. Hannah emptied her piggy bank to see how much money was in it. She had 2 quarters, a dime, a nickel and 7 pennies. How much money did Hannah have?

72¢

2. Karen had five coins. They equaled $.17. What were the five coins she had?

3 nickels, 2 pennies

3. Linda's mom emptied the change in her purse. She gave Linda 3 dimes, 2 quarters and 4 nickels for her allowance. How much was Linda's allowance?

$1

4. Daniel found a penny, a nickel and a dime on the floor of the car. How much money did he find?

16¢

5. Eddie asked for 4 quarters for parking money. How much money did he want?

$1

Value of Coins

6. Gina found five coins on the street. They totaled $.33. What coins did she find?

1 quarter, 1 nickel, 3 pennies

7. The small jar was filled with coins. Whomever came closest to guessing how much change was in the jar won all of it. Spencer won. When he emptied the jar, there were 3 quarters, 7 dimes, 5 nickels and 17 pennies. How much money did Spencer get?

$1.87

8. Mrs. Jones gave each boy $.25. She gave Tommy one coin and David three coins. What coin did Tommy get and what coins did David get?

Tommy - 1 quarter; David - 2 dimes, 1 nickel

9. When Sally paid for her candy bar with a dollar, the cashier gave her a quarter, 2 dimes and 3 pennies in change. How much did Sally get back?

48¢

10. Write different ways to make change for $.50 using the number of coins called for in each box below.

2 coins	5 coins	10 coins	4 coins	14 coins
2 quarters	5 dimes	10 nickels	1 quarter, 2 dimes, 1 nickel	9 nickels, 5 pennies

---

LET'S GO SHOPPING!

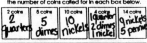

TO MALL

1. Sam was saving money from his allowance each week to buy a basketball. Last week, he put $1.74 in his bank. This week, he saved $1.59. How much money has Sam saved?

$3.33

2. Katie bought a game. It cost $2.50. She gave the cashier $3.00. How much change did she get back?

50¢

3. Maggie went to a movie. She paid $2.00 for her ticket, $1.25 for popcorn and $.75 for a drink. How much did Maggie spend at the movies?

$4.00

4. Mother bought Jack a T-shirt for $8.88 and a pair of socks for $1.99. How much did she spend for Jack's clothes?

$10.87

Addition and Subtraction of Money

5. Dinner at the restaurant cost $7.63. Mr. Jacobs gave the waiter $9.00. How much change did he get back?

$1.37

6. At the garage sale, Larry bought an old hammer for $.75, scraps of wood for $1.60 and a saw for $1.75. How much money did he spend?

$4.10

7. Joe saw a kite he wanted. It cost $9.75. He only had $5.32. How much more money must Joe get before he can buy the kite?

$4.43

8. Mother bought chicken for $6.89 and hamburger meat for $3.97. How much more did the chicken cost?

$2.92

9. Jane and Joy had lunch. Jane's lunch cost $3.15. Joy's cost $2.55. How much did their lunches cost all together?

$5.70

10. Tim spent $2.98 on craft supplies and flowers. He decorated used bottles and filled each one with water and a flower. He sold the vases with flowers for $7.00. How much money did Tim make?

$4.02

FAMILY REUNION

1. The Bell family was having a reunion in Chicago. Aunt Susie and cousins Jim and Joe left the St. Louis airport at 1:00 p.m. and arrived in Chicago at 2:30 p.m. How long was their trip?

1½ hours

2. Grandma and Grandpa Bell came from Dallas. Their plane left at noon and arrived in Chicago at 4:00 p.m. How long was their flight?

4 hours

3. Was the flight from Chicago or Dallas longer? How much longer?

Dallas - 2½ hours

4. Several family members came from Newark. They should have left at 7:30 a.m., but because of bad weather, they left 3 hours late. What time did they depart from Newark?

10:30 a.m.

5. It was a 2½ hour flight from Newark to Chicago. What time did the plane arrive in Chicago?

1 p.m.

Addition and Subtraction of Time

6. The 47 Bell family members met for dinner in Chicago at the hotel at 6:00 p.m. Because there were so many of them, it took 3½ hours to complete the meal. What time was dinner over?

9:30 p.m.

7. The next day, everyone met in the lobby at 10:00 a.m. They took a ½-hour bus ride to the zoo. They spent 3 hours at the zoo before they got back on the bus to go back to the hotel. How long were they away from the hotel?

4 hours

8. What time in the afternoon did they get back to the hotel?

2 p.m.

9. Some of the children went to a movie that started at 2:30 p.m. It was over at 5:00 p.m. How long did they have to get ready for dinner at 7:00 p.m.?

2 hours

10. Aunt Susie and cousins Jim and Joe decided to drive back to St. Louis. They left Chicago at 3:00 p.m. in a rental car. It was a 4 hour drive plus a ½-hour stop for dinner. What time did they get home? How much longer was their trip home?

9:30 p.m. - 5 hours

ARE WE THERE YET?

1. Margie left her house at 10:30 a.m. It was a 20-minute walk to Sue's house. At what time did she get to Sue's?

10:50 a.m.

2. Jill arrived at her grandmother's house at 6:05 p.m. It had taken her 35 minutes to get there. What time did Jill leave home?

5:30 p.m.

3. School starts at 8:45 a.m. Julie lives 10 minutes from school. What time should she leave so she won't be tardy?

8:35 a.m.

4. Leo left his office at 5:35 p.m. He got home at 6:15 p.m. How long did it take him to get home?

40 min.

5. Sonny went on a hike up the mountain. He started out at 9:15 a.m. and didn't get back down until noon. How long was he gone?

2 hrs, 45 min.

6. Donny and his parents left on their vacation early in the morning. They drove for 2 hours and 15 minutes before they stopped for breakfast at 8:15 a.m. What time did they leave their house?

6:00 a.m.

Time

7. Harry took a bus downtown. It took him 45 minutes. He got on the bus at 4:10 p.m. What time did he get downtown?

4:55 p.m.

8. Charles ran around the block. He began at 9:35 a.m. and finished at 9:40 a.m. How long did it take Charles to run around the block?

5 min.

9. The trip to the farm seemed to take forever. The students left at 8:10 a.m. They got to the farm at 9:15 a.m. How long did it take to get to the farm?

1 hr, 5 min.

10. Melanie stopped by Dottie's at 7:40 a.m. to pick her up for school. She had to wait 15 minutes for Dottie to finish her breakfast. What time did they leave for school?

7:55 a.m.

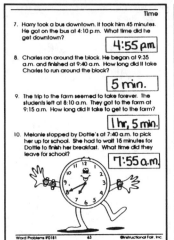

THE GREEN GROCER

1. Mr. Max, the grocer, arranged the heads of lettuce in 4 rows. He put 3 heads in each row. How many heads of lettuce were there all together?

12

2. Mrs. Brown filled each of 5 bags with 2 lemons. How many lemons did she buy?

10

3. Martha Ann selected red apples, green apples and yellow apples. She selected 3 of each kind. How many apples in all did she select?

9

4. Mr. Max put 5 asparagus stalks together in bunches. When he finished, he had 5 bunches of asparagus. How many stalks were there all together?

25

Multiplication 1-5

5. Mrs. Howard bought one of 3 different kinds of melons. How many melons did she buy?

3

6. Missy selected 5 bunches of grapes. There were 4 grapes in each bunch. How many grapes did Missy have all together?

20

7. Mr. Hare bought 4 bunches of carrots. There were 4 carrots in each bunch. How many carrots did he buy in all?

16

8. Mr. Max arranged the heads of cauliflower in 3 rows. He put 5 in each row. How many heads of cauliflower were there?

15

9. Mr. Max had to throw away 2 baskets, each containing 4 tomatoes which had rotted. How many tomatoes did he throw away in all?

8

10. Mr. Max stood 3 pineapples in a row. He had 2 rows. How many pineapples were there all together?

6

A HOT HOLIDAY CELEBRATION

1. On the 4th of July, 2 rows of drum majors, with 4 in each row, led the band down Main Street. How many drum majors led the band?

8

2. The scout troop marched in the parade. Flags were carried by 4 rows of scouts with 6 in each row. How many flags were there?

24

3. The city council followed the scouts in 2 rows of 5 each. How many people were on the city council?

10

4. Some children decorated their bikes with flags and streamers. They rode in 5 rows with 3 bikes in each row. How many decorated bikes were there?

15

Multiplication 1-6

5. The band played 6 different marches. It played each march 5 times. How many marches did the band play in all?

30

6. The parade was followed by a picnic at the park. There were 6 tables set with red, white and blue tablecloths. Six people sat at each table. How many people ate at the tables?

36

7. In the afternoon, the children got into 5 teams and ran races. There were 4 children on each team. How many children ran in the races?

20

8. When it began to get dark, 2 boys each set off 6 firecrackers. How many firecrackers were set off?

12

9. The mayor sent 4 different-colored rockets into the air. He set up 3 of each of these colors. How many rockets did the mayor put into the sky?

12

10. Three cleanup crews with 3 people in each one put the park back in order after everyone went home. How many people helped clean up?

9

TEDDY BEAR'S PICNIC

1. Eight girls arranged a picnic for their teddy bears. Each girl brought 2 teddy bears. How many teddy bears were at the picnic?

16

2. Each of the 8 girls brought 4 balloons to the picnic. How many balloons were there all together?

32

3. Patty bought 6 packages of paper plates. There were 8 plates in each package. How many plates did she buy?

48

4. Wendy bought 5 packages of napkins. There were 8 in each package. How many napkins did she buy?

40

Multiplication 2-9

5. Each of 6 girls spread honey on 9 crackers. How many crackers with honey did they serve?

54

6. Three of the girls each brought 6 yellow gummy bears. How many yellow gummy bears were there?

18

7. Five brown teddy bears each got 7 red gummy bears. How many red gummy bears were there?

35

8. Apple juice was served at the picnic. Each of 3 girls poured 9 glasses of juice. How many glasses of juice were there?

27

9. Maggie and Vicki made bear cookies. They arranged them in 9 rows with 7 in each row. How many cookies were there?

63

10. When it was time for the guests to leave, the girls gave each guest a 4-page book of bear stickers with 7 bears on each page. How many bear stickers were in each book?

28

FAR OUT

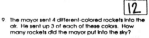

1. There were 5 astronauts in the space station already in space. Seven more came on a spaceship. How many astronauts were in space?

12

2. Reports of U.F.O. sightings were coming in from all over. The majority, 14, were sighted in the north. Two others were sighted in the south. How many more were sighted in the north?

12

3. The boys saw 8 stars in each of 3 constellations. How many stars did they see all together?

24

4. Only one astronaut went on the first flight in space. Now as many as 8 can travel in a spaceship at one time. How many more can travel in space now?

7

Choosing the Operation

5. Scientists observed 8 comets last year and only 5 this year. How many comets did they see in both years?

13

6. The lunar eclipse began at 10:10 p.m. It lasted for one hour and 20 minutes. At what time was the eclipse over?

11:30 pm

7. Some scientists believe they saw 52 meteors and others believe they saw 27. How many more did one group supposedly see than the other?

25

8. Each of 5 spaceships held 6 astronauts. How many astronauts were ready to fly into space?

30

9. The solar eclipse began at 2:13 in the afternoon and was over at 3:51 p.m. How long did the eclipse last?

1 hr, 38 min.

10. The 6 astronauts took turns sleeping during their trip in space. Each one slept 4 hours every day while in space. The astronauts were gone 8 days. How many hours did each astronaut sleep on the trip?

32

Tutor's Guide IF0181   H   ©Instructional Fair, Inc.

Two-Digit Subtraction with Borrowing

7. Of the 94 cottonwood and willow trees that lined the banks of the stream, 45 of them were cottonwoods. How many were willow trees?

8. The fisherman was out in his boat all day. He had 42 "bites," but he caught only 5 fish. How many of his "bites" got away or were not fish?

9. Nathan had 33 fish in his aquarium. He especially liked the 14 fish with bright colors. How many fish did he have that were not brightly colored?

10. Seventy-four seagulls sat on the pier that stretched out into the lake. When a large school of fish swam past, 59 seagulls flew after them. How many seagulls remained on their perches on the pier?

CARNIVAL FUN

1. There were 23 shows and 15 games at the carnival. How many activities were at the carnival?

2. Benjamin tried to win a basketball by throwing 2 beanbags. He got 25 points with the first bag he threw and 37 with the second. How many points did Benjamin get?

3. Gordie worked at the snow cone booth. He served 54 grape snow cones and 31 lemon snow cones. How many more grape snow cones did he serve?

4. There were 14 elephants and 23 monkeys in the animal show. How many animals were in the show?

5. Peter started out with 25 tickets. Within the first hour, he had used 17 of them. How many tickets did he have left?

6. The merry-go-round could hold 56 people. There were 44 on it. How many more people could get on the merry-go-round?

Two-Digit Addition and Subtraction

7. Two small cars drove into the tent. Sixteen clowns got out of one car; 22 got out of the other car. How many clowns got out of the cars?

8. Jamie took a guess at how many candies were in the jar. He guessed 57. There were 76. By how many did Jamie miss the correct number?

9. There were 37 white mice and 12 black mice in the mouse show. How many mice were in the mouse show?

10. Taylor played the dart game. He started with 99 points. The object of the game was to get down to zero. He threw 3 darts for a total of 67 points. How many more points did he need to get to zero?

ECOLOGY COUNT

1. John and Mike collected used newspapers in their neighborhood for the paper drive. John brought in 253 pounds of paper, and Mike brought in 144 pounds. How many pounds of paper did they collect altogether?

2. Trees are used to make paper. One tree could make 700 paper grocery bags. What could 2 trees make?

3. Mr. Glasser's and Miss Miller's classes saved all the plastic food packages their families bought during the year. Mr. Glasser's class had 192 pounds. Miss Miller's class had 206 pounds. How much plastic packaging did they have altogether?

4. While riding in the car, Murray counted 256 pieces of trash along the roadside on the first day of his vacation. His brother counted 223 pieces the second day. How many pieces of trash did they count altogether?

5. The sixth grade separated the plastic and glass bottles and jars they collected. The sixth-graders counted 121 glass containers and 352 plastic ones. How many bottles and jars did they collect?

6. Katie and her family used 175 feet of paper towels one week. The next week, they tried to use less. They only used 122 feet. How many feet of paper towels did they use both weeks?

7. Martin and Harris saved all the junk mail delivered to their homes in a month. Martin got 216 pieces of junk mail. Harris got 310. How many pieces of junk mail did they receive altogether?

8. Teri counted the number of times her refrigerator door was opened every day. At the end of the month, it had been opened 506 times. Loni did the same at her house and found hers was opened 483 times. How many times were their refrigerator doors opened altogether?

9. By letting the water run when she washed the dishes, Mother wasted at least 210 gallons of water in a week. How many gallons of water did she waste in 2 weeks?

WEIGH IN

1. The total weight of the boys in the class was 952 pounds. The total weight of the girls was 770. What was the total weight of the class?

2. Mrs. Joseph, the principal, weighed 137 pounds. Her secretary weighed 115. What did they weigh together?

3. The school nurse made a chart with the total weight of each grade level. The first grade weighed 968 pounds, and the kindergarten weighed 857 pounds. How much did the grade levels weigh together?

4. Mrs. Leap's room collected 206 pounds of newspaper, and Mrs. Bound's room collected 329 pounds. How many pounds of paper did the rooms collect altogether?

Three-Digit Addition with Carrying

5. The boxers weighed in before their match. One weighed 404 pounds. The other weighed 397 pounds. How much did they weigh together?

6. The mother elephant had 2 babies. One weighed 105 pounds. The other weighed 109 pounds. How much did the babies weigh altogether?

7. The mother bear weighed 927 pounds. Her cub weighed 143 pounds. How much did they weigh altogether?

8. The zoo used 550 pounds of hay just for the elephants in a day. How much did they use in two days?

9. The pet store sold 156 pounds of dog food in the morning and 191 pounds in the afternoon. How much dog food did the store sell all day?

10. The pet store had 109 pounds of dog food left. The store ordered 959 pounds more. How much would it then have altogether?

CROWD CONTROL

1. The movie theater held only 785 people. There were 995 people wanting to see the movie. How many people did the theater have to turn away?

2. The pet store had 566 mice. There were only enough cages for 450. How many mice did the store have to give away?

3. The dog and cat shelter had 678 animals. The shelter really could hold only 425 at a time. For how many dogs and cats did they need to quickly find homes?

4. In the low part of the forest, 825 trees were crowded together so that none of them were growing very well. The forest service moved 304 of the trees to other parts of the forest. How many trees remained in the low part?

Three-Digit Subtraction Without Borrowing

5. After the football game, 473 excited fans ran onto the field. The ushers had to remove 162 of them who were tearing down the goal posts. How many fans got to remain on the field?

6. Trucks came to the feed lot to pick up some of the 975 cattle waiting to be shipped to market. The trucks were able to take all but 152 of the cattle. How many cattle went on the trucks?

7. The store counted 879 shirts when it took inventory. The store decided to put 354 of them on sale. How many shirts did not go on sale?

8. One day, the library checked out 315 books and checked in 568 returns. How many more books were returned than checked out?

9. The museum guards let in only 125 people of the 686 waiting in line to see the exhibit. How many people were still in line?

10. There were 156 new cars available and 266 buyers. How many buyers had to wait for the next shipment of cars?

MAXIMUM AND MINIMUM

1. The sign on the bridge read, "No more than 150 people may stand on this bridge at one time." There were 203 people on it. How many people had to get off the bridge?

2. When James hit the muscle machine with a sledge hammer, the bell went off because he got the most points possible—990. Harvey got only 399 points. How many more points did James get than Harvey?

3. The highest building in downtown Higginsville had 810 steps from the ground floor to the fortieth floor on top. The shortest building had only 125 steps. How many more steps did the tallest building have than the shortest?

4. Toby read the most pages, 946, during free reading time. Stan read the least, 209. How many more pages did Toby read than Stan?

5. While practicing for the race, Jack kept a record of how long it took him to run 26 miles. His best time was 390 minutes. His worst time was 425 minutes. What is the difference between his best and worst times?

Three-Digit Subtraction with Borrowing

6. The highest hill in the park is 352 inches high. The smallest hill is 196 inches high. What is the difference in height between the two hills?

7. The students at Central School were saving energy. They had a contest to see who walked the most miles. Greg won. He walked 437 miles. Louis walked the least. He walked 59 miles. What was the difference between the boys' miles?

8. Theo raised the most money, $8.27, for the class' present to the school. Penny raised the least, $1.59. What was the difference between the amounts?

9. The grade level with the most students was sixth grade. It had 305 students. The grade level with the least number of students was second grade. It had 269. How many less students are in the second grade.

10. The largest factory in town had 685 people working in it. The smallest factory had 96. What is the difference in the number of people employed in the largest and smallest factories?

OVER THE RIVER AND THROUGH THE WOODS

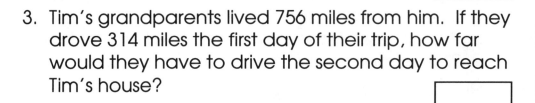

OCEAN
356 miles

1. On the first day of the Diamonds' vacation to the ocean, they drove 427 miles. On the second day, they drove 356 miles. How far was the ocean from their home?

2. The furniture left the factory on a freight train. It traveled 605 miles before it was put on a truck. The truck drove it 419 miles to the store. How far did the furniture travel until it reached its destination?

3. Tim's grandparents lived 756 miles from him. If they drove 314 miles the first day of their trip, how far would they have to drive the second day to reach Tim's house?

4. The Murrays and Sheelines were friends, but they lived far apart. They decided to meet in a city almost halfway between them. The Murrays drove 389 miles, and the Sheelines drove 398 miles. How many miles apart did they live?

Three-Digit Addition and Subtraction

5. The train had to travel 890 miles. It had gone 512 miles. How much farther did it have to go?

6. The Bakers had 692 miles to travel. They stopped for lunch after going 293 miles. How many miles did they have to go after lunch?

7. Mrs. Saff drove 129 miles, and her husband drove 205 miles. How far did they drive altogether?

8. The airplane was scheduled to land once before it reached its destination of Chicago which was 545 miles away. It landed in St. Louis after flying 255 miles. How many more miles did the plane have to travel before it arrived in Chicago?

9. The three-day cruise was 744 miles. The ship's last stop was 578 miles from its final port. How many miles did the ship have left to travel?

10. Lenny drove back and forth to work five days a week for a total of 192 miles. His boss drove a total of 180 miles a week. How many miles did they drive altogether?

BIG, BIGGER, BIGGEST

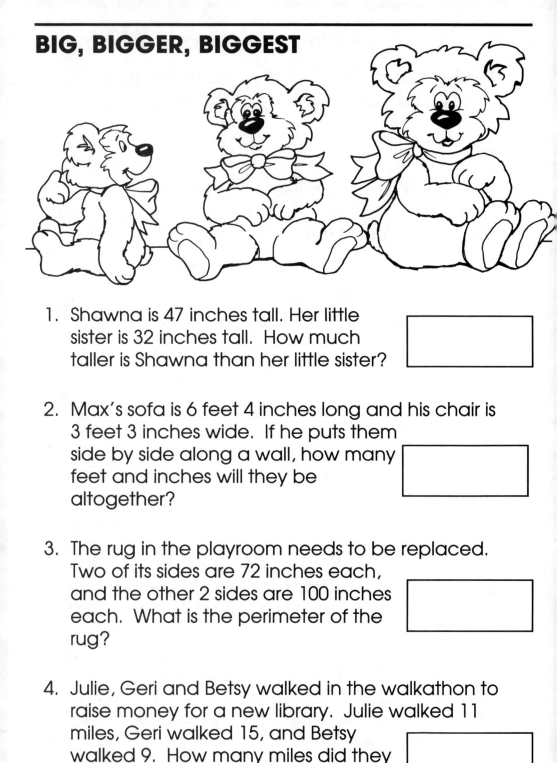

1. Shawna is 47 inches tall. Her little sister is 32 inches tall. How much taller is Shawna than her little sister?

2. Max's sofa is 6 feet 4 inches long and his chair is 3 feet 3 inches wide. If he puts them side by side along a wall, how many feet and inches will they be altogether?

3. The rug in the playroom needs to be replaced. Two of its sides are 72 inches each, and the other 2 sides are 100 inches each. What is the perimeter of the rug?

4. Julie, Geri and Betsy walked in the walkathon to raise money for a new library. Julie walked 11 miles, Geri walked 15, and Betsy walked 9. How many miles did they walk altogether?

Addition and Subtraction Using Measurement

5. Andy weighed 45 pounds last year and was 3 feet 5 inches tall. When he was measured this year, he weighed 59 pounds and was 3 feet 10 inches tall. How many pounds did he gain and how many inches did he grow in one year?

6. Aaron weighed more than anyone else in the class. He weighed 87 pounds. Meg weighed the least. She weighed 46 pounds. What was the difference in their weights?

7. If today were the sixth of October, how many days would it be until the eighteenth?

8. The first of April is on a Sunday. What will the date of the next Sunday be?

9. In the morning, the temperature was 32 degrees. In the afternoon, it rose to 60 degrees. How many degrees warmer was it in the afternoon?

10. There are 2 cups in a pint. There are 2 pints in a quart. How many cups are in a quart?

SPRING CONCERT

1. There were 6 violins, 4 cellos and 2 bass instruments in the string section of the orchestra. How many string instruments were in the orchestra?

2. There were 2 tubas, 4 trombones and 4 trumpets in the brass section. How many instruments were in the brass section?

3. The woodwind section had 6 clarinet players, 3 oboe players and 5 bassoon players. How many players were in the woodwind section?

4. The percussion section was the smallest section but perhaps the loudest. It had 1 piano, 2 drums and 1 tambourine. How many instruments were in the percussion section of the orchestra?

Three Single-Digit Addends

5. The singers in the first row held 7 tulips, 5 daisies and 8 roses. How many flowers were held by the singers in the first row?

6. The girls wore light-colored dresses. Eight wore pink, 9 wore yellow and 9 wore light blue. How many girls wore light-colored dresses?

7. The program listed 3 dances, 8 songs and 7 musical pieces to be performed. How many items were listed on the program?

8. The first dance took 3 minutes, the second took 5 minutes, and the last dance took 3 minutes. How many minutes in all were the dances?

9. There were refreshments after the concert. Carrie had 3 cookies, her brother had 3, and her mom had 2. How many cookies did Carrie and her family eat?

10. The boys in the chorus had 9 glasses of grape juice, 9 glasses of lemonade and 9 glasses of punch. How many drinks did the boys have in all?

COUNTING ON VACATION

1. The Cutlers traveled by car to visit Grandma. Mother packed 12 pairs of jeans, 24 T-shirts and 10 sweaters for the family. How many things did she pack?

2. Lawrence Cutler amused himself on the trip by counting out-of-state license plates. He saw 11 from New Mexico, 12 from Colorado and 10 from Arizona. How many license plates did Lawrence count?

3. Nan Cutler counted the number of farm animals she saw. She counted 35 cows, 12 horses and 15 pigs. How many farm animals did she count?

4. In the first hour, the Cutlers traveled 45 miles. In the second hour, they traveled 52 miles. In the third hour, they traveled 16 miles. How many miles did they travel?

5. The Cutlers filled the car with 18 gallons of gas before they left home. They filled it again with 15 gallons and again with 17 gallons. With how many gallons in all did they fill the car on the trip.

6. Lawrence swam laps in his grandmother's pool. One day, he swam 16 laps. The next day, he swam 21 laps, and the last day, he swam 33 laps. How many laps did Lawrence swim in all?

7. Nan helped Grandma bake cookies. They made 46 sugar cookies, 36 chocolate cookies and 25 butter cookies. How many cookies did they make?

8. Every day, the Cutlers had family time. They read for 60 minutes. They talked for 25 minutes, and they played a game for 45 minutes. Family time lasted how many minutes?

9. The Cutler family took a short side trip. They drove 41 miles to the ocean. Then they drove along the coast for 14 miles. The trip back to Grandma's house was 48 miles. How many miles in all was their side trip?

COUNTING MONEY

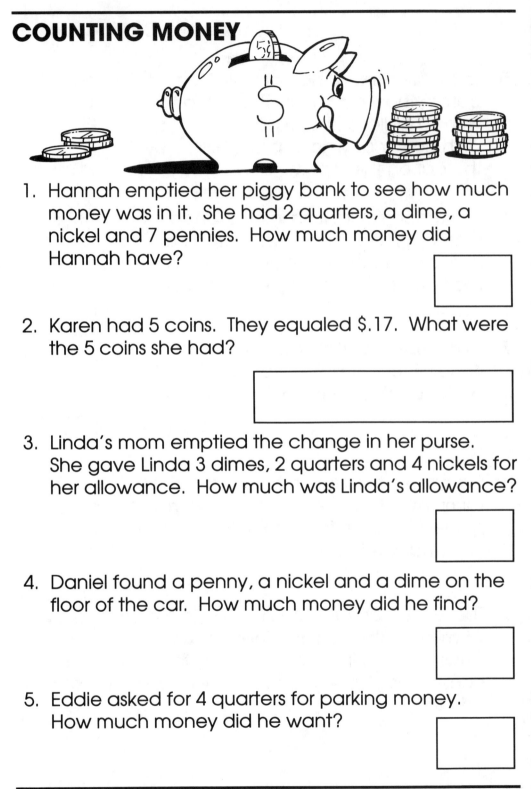

1. Hannah emptied her piggy bank to see how much money was in it. She had 2 quarters, a dime, a nickel and 7 pennies. How much money did Hannah have?

2. Karen had 5 coins. They equaled $.17. What were the 5 coins she had?

3. Linda's mom emptied the change in her purse. She gave Linda 3 dimes, 2 quarters and 4 nickels for her allowance. How much was Linda's allowance?

4. Daniel found a penny, a nickel and a dime on the floor of the car. How much money did he find?

5. Eddie asked for 4 quarters for parking money. How much money did he want?

6. Gina found 5 coins on the street. They totaled $.33. What coins did she find?

7. The small jar was filled with coins. Whomever came closest to guessing how much change was in the jar won all of it. Spencer won. When he emptied the jar, there were 3 quarters, 7 dimes, 5 nickels and 17 pennies. How much money did Spencer get?

8. Mrs. Jones gave each boy $.25. She gave Tommy 1 coin and David 3 coins. What coin did Tommy get and what coins did David get?

9. When Sally paid for her candy bar with a dollar, the cashier gave her a quarter, 2 dimes and 3 pennies in change. How much did Sally get back?

10. Write different ways to make change for $.50 using the number of coins shown in each box below.

2 coins	5 coins	10 coins	4 coins	14 coins

LET'S GO SHOPPING!

1. Sam was saving money from his allowance each week to buy a basketball. Last week, he put $1.74 in his bank. This week, he saved $1.59. How much money has Sam saved?

2. Katie bought a game. It cost $2.50. She gave the cashier $3.00. How much change did she get back?

3. Maggie went to a movie. She paid $2.00 for her ticket, $1.25 for popcorn and $.75 for a drink. How much did Maggie spend at the movie?

4. Mother bought Jack a T-shirt for $8.88 and a pair of socks for $1.99. How much did she spend for Jack's clothes?

Addition and Subtraction of Money

5. Dinner at the restaurant cost $7.63. Mr. Jacobs gave the waiter $9.00. How much change did he get back?

6. At the garage sale, Larry bought an old hammer for $.75, scraps of wood for $1.60 and a saw for $1.75. How much money did he spend?

7. Joe saw a kite he wanted. It cost $9.75. He only had $5.32. How much more money must Joe get before he can buy the kite?

8. Mother bought chicken for $6.89 and hamburger meat for $3.97. How much more did the chicken cost?

9. Jane and Joy had lunch. Jane's lunch cost $3.15. Joy's cost $2.55. How much did their lunches cost altogether?

10. Tim spent $2.98 on craft supplies and flowers. He decorated used bottles and filled each one with water and a flower. He sold all of the vases with flowers for $7.00. How much profit did Tim make?

FAMILY REUNION

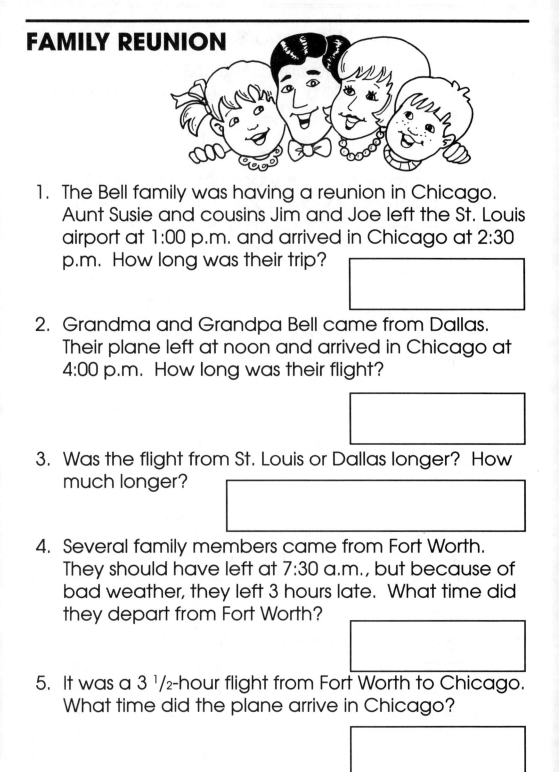

1. The Bell family was having a reunion in Chicago. Aunt Susie and cousins Jim and Joe left the St. Louis airport at 1:00 p.m. and arrived in Chicago at 2:30 p.m. How long was their trip?

2. Grandma and Grandpa Bell came from Dallas. Their plane left at noon and arrived in Chicago at 4:00 p.m. How long was their flight?

3. Was the flight from St. Louis or Dallas longer? How much longer?

4. Several family members came from Fort Worth. They should have left at 7:30 a.m., but because of bad weather, they left 3 hours late. What time did they depart from Fort Worth?

5. It was a 3 1/2-hour flight from Fort Worth to Chicago. What time did the plane arrive in Chicago?

Addition and Subtraction of Time

6. The 47 Bell family members met for dinner in Chicago at the hotel at 6:00 p.m. Because there were so many of them, it took $3\frac{1}{2}$ hours to complete the meal. At what time was dinner over?

7. The next day, everyone met in the lobby at 10:00 a.m. They took a $\frac{1}{2}$-hour bus ride to the zoo. They spent 3 hours at the zoo before they got back on the bus to go back to the hotel. How long were they away from the hotel?

8. What time in the afternoon did they get back to the hotel?

9. Some of the children went to a movie that started at 2:30 p.m. It was over at 5:00 p.m. How long did they have to get ready for dinner at 7:00 p.m?

10. Aunt Susie and cousins Jim and Joe decided to drive back to St. Louis. They left Chicago at 3:00 p.m. in a rental car. It was a 6-hour drive plus a $\frac{1}{2}$-hour stop for dinner. What time did they get home?

ARE WE THERE YET?

1. Margie left her house at 10:30 a.m. It was a 20-minute walk to Sue's house. At what time did she get to Sue's?

2. Jill arrived at her grandmother's house at 6:05 p.m. It had taken her 35 minutes to get there. At what time did Jill leave home?

3. School starts at 8:45 a.m. Julie lives 10 minutes from school. At what time should she leave home so she won't be tardy?

4. Leo left his office at 5:35 p.m. He got home at 6:15 p.m. How long did it take him to get home?

5. Sonny went on a hike up the mountain. He started out at 9:15 a.m. and did not get back down until noon. How long was he gone?

6. Donny and his parents left on their vacation early in the morning. They drove for 2 hours and 15 minutes before they stopped for breakfast at 8:15 a.m. At what time did they leave their house?

7. Harry took a bus downtown. It took him 45 minutes. He got on the bus at 4:10 p.m. At what time did he get downtown?

8. Charles ran around the block. He began at 9:35 a.m. and finished at 9:40 a.m. How long did it take Charles to run around the block?

9. The trip to the farm seemed to take forever. The students left at 8:10 a.m. They got to the farm at 9:15 a.m. How long did it take to get to the farm?

10. Melanie stopped by Dottie's house at 7:40 a.m. to pick her up for school. She had to wait 15 minutes for Dottie to finish her breakfast. At what time did they leave for school?

THE GREEN GROCER

1. Mr. Max, the grocer, arranged the heads of lettuce in 4 rows. He put 3 heads in each row. How many heads of lettuce were there altogether?

2. Mrs. Brown filled each of 5 bags with 2 lemons. How many lemons did she buy?

3. Martha Ann selected red apples, green apples and yellow apples. She selected 3 of each kind. How many apples in all did she select?

4. Mr. Max put 5 asparagus stalks together in bunches. When he finished, he had 5 bunches of asparagus. How many stalks were there altogether?

5. Mrs. Howard bought one of 3 different kinds of melons. How many melons did she buy?

6. Missy selected 5 bunches of grapes. There were 4 grapes in each bunch. How many grapes did Missy have altogether?

7. Mr. Hare bought 4 bunches of carrots. There were 4 carrots in each bunch. How many carrots did he buy in all?

8. Mr. Max arranged the heads of cauliflower in 3 rows. He put 5 in each row. How many heads of cauliflower were there?

9. Mr. Max had to throw away 2 baskets, each containing 4 tomatoes which had rotted. How many tomatoes did he throw away in all?

10. Mr. Max stood 3 pineapples in a row. He had 2 rows. How many pineapples were there altogether?

A HOT HOLIDAY CELEBRATION

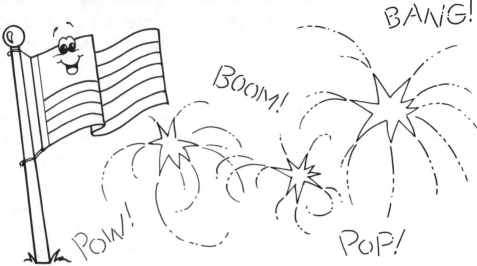

1. On the 4th of July, 2 rows of drum majors, with 4 in each row, led the band down Main Street. How many drum majors led the band?

2. The scout troop marched in the parade. Flags were carried by 4 rows of scouts with 6 in each row. How many flags were there?

3. The city council followed the scouts in 2 rows of 5 each. How many people were on the city council?

4. Some children decorated their bikes with flags and streamers. They rode in 5 rows with 3 bikes in each row. How many decorated bikes were there?

5. The band played 6 different marches. It played each march 5 times. How many marches did the band play in all?

6. The parade was followed by a picnic at the park. There were 6 tables set with red, white and blue tablecloths. Six people sat at each table. How many people ate at the tables?

7. In the afternoon, the children got into 5 teams and ran races. There were 4 children on each team. How many children ran in the races?

8. When it began to get dark, 2 boys each set off 6 firecrackers. How many firecrackers were set off?

9. The mayor sent 4 different-colored rockets into the air. He sent up 3 of each color. How many rockets did the mayor put into the sky?

10. Three cleanup crews with 3 people in each one put the park back in order after everyone went home. How many people helped clean up?

TEDDY BEARS' PICNIC

1. Eight girls arranged a picnic for their teddy bears. Each girl brought 2 teddy bears. How many teddy bears were at the picnic?

2. Each of the 8 girls brought 4 balloons to the picnic. How many balloons were there altogether?

3. Patty bought 6 packages of paper plates. There were 8 plates in each package. How many plates did she buy?

4. Wendy bought 5 packages of napkins. There were 8 in each package. How many napkins did she buy?

5. Each of 6 girls spread honey on 9 crackers. How many crackers with honey did they serve?

6. Three of the girls each brought 6 yellow gummy bears. How many yellow gummy bears were there?

7. Five brown teddy bears each got 7 red gummy bears. How many red gummy bears were there?

8. Apple juice was served at the picnic. Each of 3 girls poured 9 glasses of juice. How many glasses of juice were there?

9. Maggie and Vicki made bear cookies. They arranged them in 9 rows with 7 in each row. How many cookies were there?

10. When it was time for the guests to leave, the girls gave each guest a 4-page book of bear stickers with 7 bears on each page. How many bear stickers were in each book?

FAR OUT

1. There were 5 astronauts in the space station already in space. Seven more came on a spaceship. How many astronauts were in space?

2. Reports of U.F.O. sightings were coming in from many places. The majority, 14, were sighted in the north. Two others were sighted in the south. How many more were sighted in the north?

3. The boys saw 8 stars in each of 3 constellations. How many stars did they see altogether?

4. Only 1 astronaut went on the first flight in space. Now as many as 8 can travel in a spaceship at one time. How many more can travel in space now?

Choosing the Operation

5. Scientists observed 8 comets last year and only 5 this year. How many comets did they see in both years?

6. The lunar eclipse began at 10:10 p.m. It lasted for one hour and 20 minutes. At what time did the eclipse end?

7. Some scientists believe they saw 52 meteors and others believe they saw 27. How many more did one group supposedly see than the other?

8. Each of 5 spaceships held 6 astronauts. How many astronauts were ready to fly into space?

9. The solar eclipse began at 2:13 in the afternoon and ended at 3:51 p.m. How long did the eclipse last?

10. The 6 astronauts took turns sleeping during their trip in space. Each one slept 4 hours every day while in space. The astronauts were gone 8 days. How many hours did each astronaut sleep on the trip?

HELP-AT-HOME ACTIVITIES

Below are some activities to do with your child at home.

1. Make "Family Graphs" with your child. Make a graph of everyone's height, weight and/or age. When the graphs are complete, your child can find the differences between family members in each variable.

2. Look at the day's date on a calendar. Your child can determine what the date will be 2 days, 7 days and 12 days from now. Or, determine what the date was 3 days ago, 8 days ago, etc.

3. Put price tags on various items in your home. Give your child real or play money and have him/her make the exact amount for each item.

4. Make a list of specific activities and the times these activities will take place. Ask your child to tell how long before each event occurs, how long it is between events, etc.

5. Play a finger game. You and your child each hold up any number of fingers simultaneously on a given signal. Add the numbers together or find the difference between the number of fingers held up.

6. Use peanuts to make subtraction problems. Let your child eat the differences as a reward for a correct answer.

7. Cut out pictures of groups of people and/or animals from old books, magazines or newspapers. Have your child make up story problems about them.

8. Measure small areas (i.e. tabletops, book covers, desks, etc.) together. Have your child draw a picture of each and write the measurements along each appropriate side.

9. Have your child count by 2's, 5's and 10's to 100.

10. Your child can use holiday themes to make up word problems. (Example: Twelve guests came to the Thanksgiving feast. Six dressed like Indians. How many dressed like Pilgrims?)

11. Help your child collect and then use items from nature (sticks, leaves, pebbles) to make up word problems.

12. Play "Around the House" math. For example, your child can count the number of chairs in 2 different rooms. Then, he/she can make up a problem that tells something about them.